DATE DUE

DEATH AT MIDNIGHT

Death at Midnight

The Confession
of an Executioner

DONALD A. CABANA

Northeastern University Press
Boston

Northeastern University Press

Library of Congress Cataloging-in-Publication Data
Cabana, Don.
    Death at midnight : the confession of an executioner / Donald A. Cabana.
        p.   cm.
    Includes index.
    ISBN 1-55553-264-0 (cloth : alk. paper)
        1. Executions and executioners—Mississippi—Case studies.
    2. Capital punishment—Mississippi—Case studies. 3. Capital
    punishment—Moral and ethical aspects. 4. Prison wardens—
    Mississippi—Case studies. 5. Death row inmates—Mississippi—Case
    studies. I. Title.
    HV8694.C225   1996
    364.6'6'09762—dc20   95-44967

Designed by Peter Blaiwas

Composed in Stempel Schneidler by Northeastern Graphic Services, Inc., Hackensack, New Jersey. Printed and bound by Edwards Brothers, Inc., Ann Arbor, Michigan. The paper is Glatfelter Offset, an acid-free stock.

MANUFACTURED IN THE UNITED STATES OF AMERICA
00 99 98 97 96   5 4 3 2 1

This book is dedicated

To my wife, Miriam, a mountain of strength and loyalty, and my greatest asset

To my six wonderful children, Scott Fleming, Leigh Michele, Samuel Ashley, Angela Renee, Kristin Nicole, and Christopher Walker

To my three beautiful grandchildren, Dominic Anthony, Brittany Taylor, and Joshua Matthew

To my beloved parents, all four of them, Samuel, Dorothy, Charles, and Bessie

To Connie Ray Evans and the other men and women who were entrusted to my care

And to the thousands of men and women who labor patiently in America's prisons in the belief that people can and do change

Acknowledgments

I express my heartfelt gratitude to all those who encouraged me in the writing of this book. A special tribute is due my wife, who juggled a job while raising the three of our children still at home and yet still found time to review and offer invaluable suggestions on this manuscript.

I also thank Tyler Fletcher, who offered tremendous encouragement, and my colleague Bill Taylor for his invaluable insights, expert that he is on Mississippi's penal history.

That state's commissioner of corrections, Steve Puckett, gave the most valuable of gifts, free and unrestricted access to inmates and staff at the Mississippi State Penitentiary at Parchman.

Kathleen Dennis deserves accolades extraordinaire for her unstinting duty as manuscript typist and unofficial critic. Her past experience as a corrections practitioner provided invaluable assistance and insight.

I also owe a very substantial debt of gratitude to Sheila Chandler, who rendered invaluable assistance on more than one occasion.

I thank my editor at Northeastern, Bill Frohlich, for his patience and encouragement, as well as the opportunity to tell this story.

Finally, I thank my mother and my father, who taught me to believe that all things are possible.

Contents

Preface

This book was a long time in the making, growing out of an exciting and challenging twenty-five years of service in corrections.

Capital punishment grips the imagination of contemporary America like no other issue. In the abstract, the death penalty is quickly endorsed and facilely supported by an increasingly vocal populace. For those few, however, who are actually authorized by the state to kill another human being, the death penalty becomes a chilling exposé of the darkest emotions of the citizenry.

Executions do not take place within a vacuum; rather, they result from a vast combination of interrelated social and historical factors, along with legal maneuverings. We freely presume it possible to point a finger and say, "That's why he's on death row." In doing so, however, we forget the numerous unseen forces at work that contribute to a man's final walk.

I spent most of my career as a prison administrator convinced of the need for capital punishment. I had always been something of a bureaucratic utopian, fully committed to the notion that if the government deemed capital punishment necessary then it must be so. I had forgotten to search beyond the law and political rhetoric and examine the morality of it all. Not until I was confronted with supervising and carrying out the ultimate retribution did I begin to question the process in earnest. The execution of Edward Earl Johnson served as a milestone, an event at which to pause and wonder. But it was the execution of Connie Ray Evans that became, for me, a personal moment of truth.

I am not John Grisham. I cannot promise that this book will be a thrilling or suspenseful potboiler. I did not write it with those attributes in mind. I wrote to provide an insider's look at the secretive, mysterious world of the execution chamber. Capital punishment exacts a toll on those who must carry it out. The executioner's tale, a vantage point that is seldom recognized, requires telling.

More importantly, however, this is a book about life. It is a story of two ordinary men, separated by culture, education, and life's experiences. Ultimately, Connie Ray Evans and I would bridge that gulf—forging a closeness that not even the gas chamber could interrupt. In the end, this is, more than anything else, a book that celebrates achievement. That a young black man, who had no choice but to die in a gas chamber, and a middle-aged white man, the warden who had no choice but to carry the execution to its conclusion, could have come to regard each other as friends is an achievement that is surely cause for joy and celebration.

DEATH AT MIDNIGHT

Full Circle

When you have steeled yourself, as I have, to supervise the death
of a young and healthy man; when you try, as I try,
to let routine rule while doing everything within the law
to make the end as merciful as possible, it's heartbreaking
to run against the raw of human suffering.

Lewis Lawes, Warden, Sing Sing Prison, 1932

Emerging slowly from the last-night cell into the execution room, I felt
totally alone, despite being surrounded by the sounds and smells of
preparations for death. For an instant I felt invisible, lost in the privacy
of anguished, confused thoughts, but the sounds of impending death
abruptly jarred me back to reality. Whispered exchanges of last-minute instructions among nervous staff, the clatter of turning valves, the
odor of chemicals that left a burning sensation in the nostrils—all
served as somber reminders that death loomed nearby. Turning with
a start, I slowly walked toward the chemical room, my attention focused on the eerie sound of muffled voices drifting from behind the
partially closed door. Peering through the window of the small cubi-
cle, I stared with inexplicable fascination as two men, faces hidden by
gas masks, cautiously mixed the chemicals that would soon dispense
justice and vengeance to the condemned prisoner who now maintained a lonely vigil just a few feet away.

A chill suddenly trickled down my spine; there was something
unsettling about witnessing such ghoulish preparations. I wondered if
the two men felt it too, as I pushed the door open and nervously
cleared my throat to announce my presence. The pair briefly interrupted their work, turning only slightly from the sink they were leaning over. Everything would be ready without complication, they assured me. I nodded in acknowledgment. Even though the room was

dimly lit, I could see large beads of perspiration sliding down their fore-heads to the top of the gas masks that tightly enclosed their faces. Both men bore bright red streaks on their cheeks and necks from the oppres-sive heat in the cramped room. Their breathing was labored as they worked inside cumbersome masks and rubber gloves.

Backing out of the close space, I was overcome by a wave of nau-sea. Surveying the execution room, my eyes fixed on the cold steel chair in the middle of the gas chamber. Contemplating the difficulty of watching a man die, especially when strapped in a chair while his lungs are filled with poison gas, I shook my head. What the hell was I doing here? How had my career come to this? It all seemed so unreal, yet I knew that reality was only moments away.

While the execution of Connie Ray Evans would not be my first, it would have a great deal more personal meaning for me. Reaching for the handle on the heavy steel door that separated the last-night cell from the execution room, I quickly glanced around one more time. Just to my right, two physicians were preparing the cardiac monitor that would announce the prisoner's death. To the left and behind me was a shelf secured on the back wall, with two telephones resting silently for the moment. The black phone, for inside calls only, served as a di-rect line to the witness room; the red telephone was a direct line to the Mississippi attorney general's office.

Everything seemed to be ready. An officer was fumbling with the ring of keys in his hand, anxiously trying to find the one that would unlock the metal door that led to the last-night cell. As the young guard sheepishly apologized, Deputy Warden Dwight Presley ap-proached the door. Dwight and I had been friends a long time. He was the quintessence of good humor and joviality, with a wide grin and a hearty, infectious laugh. On this night, however, not even Dwight could mask the strain that everyone on the execution team was under. His voice betrayed an unusual irritability as he advised me that all the witnesses were assembled on the other side of the chamber, in the witness room. The windows through which they would view the ex-ecution were covered by black curtains. As we discussed last-minute details, I hastily reached for the black telephone. The familiar voice on the other end was that of Steve Puckett, deputy warden in charge of prison security, to whom I had assigned responsibility for the witness room. We quickly discussed several points concerning the witnesses, things we had reviewed dozens of times already. Even though I was a bundle of nerves, I was determined not to reveal my feelings to the rest of the staff. As I hung up the phone, Dwight Presley patted me on the back, exhorting me to relax and assuring me that everything would be okay. The young officer finally opened the door to the last-night cell. As I stepped through, I turned back to Dwight, wanting to explain how difficult this one was going to be for me. He gently cut me off in midsentence, insisting that he understood and shared my feelings. Whispering a barely audible, "Thanks," I disappeared into the last-night cell.

Connie Ray Evans was sitting on the bunk. As he leaned back against the wall, he chatted calmly with the prison chaplain, Ron Padgett. It was just the three of us now—a condemned prisoner, his pastor, and the warden. While the last few moments of Evans's life ran by, we would engage in idle chatter, almost as if attempting to deny fate its wish. I scrutinized the young black man sitting just inches away and asked myself how something could go so terribly wrong in a person's life.

He was in many respects just another obscure criminal, convicted of a senseless crime of greed and violence. Connie Ray Evans arrived at prison a young man of twenty. The harvest of his ill-conceived robbery of a convenience store was two hundred dollars, one murdered clerk, and enough bitterness to fill two lifetimes. He had a partner in his crime, yet Connie received the death penalty, while the other man got twenty years, with all but five suspended. As so often happens, his co-conspirator beat a hot path to the prosecutor and turned state's evidence in exchange for an extremely lenient sentence. Although Evans readily confessed to being the triggerman, both he and his partner certainly bore culpability for capital murder. Connie never tried to excuse himself from responsibility for his role in a terrible crime. But what he could never understand was the disparity between his punishment and that of his partner. On a humid summer night six years later, only this reticent young man would pay for a heinous crime with his life. His partner had already been released from prison.

Connie Evans should have meant no more to me than any other condemned prisoner on "the row," as inmates and staff call death row, but it was not that way. In the course of almost four years, during my many visits as warden to death row, we had developed something of a relationship. Getting to know him had been a rewarding experience, and our communication with each other was something I believed we both genuinely looked forward to. Now it was all rapidly coming to an end, as the time arrived for me to give the order that would put him to death.

The Mississippi State Penitentiary gas chamber, with walls of institutional silver, sat just a few feet away. Although we could not hear the noisy preparations that were taking place just beyond the cell door, it was impossible not to feel its presence. Resembling a diving bell with

The door to Parchman's gas chamber.

windows on six sides, the grotesque structure sits ominously close to all the occupants of the row—a menacing reminder to each of them of their date with death.

If the chamber is intimidating, the death chair it contains fills one with foreboding. Constructed of steel and painted black, it is firmly bolted to the floor, precisely in the center of the chamber. The chair's seat is mesh, designed to hasten absorption of the deadly gas that envelops the victim. The death chair sits in cold blackness and silence, an aura interrupted only by the thick brown leather straps that immobilize the condemned man's legs, chest, and arms. The straps are aged and worn, their cracks offering silent testimony to the struggles of three dozen men against them since 1955.

Atop the chair sits a headrest, similar to those found on barber chairs. The device secures the prisoner's head, preventing it from thrashing around during the violent seizures that occur when he inhales the cyanide compound. Beneath the chair rests an innocuous dish into which cyanide crystals are poured. A lever located outside the chamber drops the dish of crystals into a waiting receptacle containing sulfuric acid and distilled water. These are the ingredients that create the lethal gas.

Behind the chair an iron support pipe rises to the ceiling. Its rather odd location reveals that although the chamber's architect may have designed a lethally proficient machine, he was far less concerned with the penologically correct or politically acceptable essentials of a "humane" execution protocol. When Mississippi executed Jimmy Lee Gray in 1983, the iron pipe became a center of controversy. At the time, nothing was used to immobilize the convicted child killer's head. Consequently, media representatives and other eyewitnesses to the execution reported Gray suffering a torturous death, his head flailing about wildly, smashing the metal pipe many times before he lost consciousness.

After the execution, a firestorm of criticism erupted. Gray's attorney, Dennis Balske, painted a particularly grim picture of his client's final agonizing moments in the gas chamber. And if the account rendered by the condemned man's lawyer seemed emotionally laden, what of Dan Lohwasser's description? He could hardly have been accused of having an ax to grind. A reporter for United Press International covering Gray's execution, Lohwasser happened to be one of the journalists selected to witness the actual killing. As a former helicopter pilot in Viet Nam he was no stranger to violent death, and his recollections of Jimmy Lee Gray's final moments of life were profoundly disquieting to some. When, a full eight minutes into the execution, Gray was still violently striking his head on the iron pipe, a prison official suddenly escorted the witnesses out of the viewing room. They observed that Jimmy Lee Gray was still alive and struggling for air.

Carrying out an execution can hardly be described as a pleasant task, but an execution gone awry is something no warden wants to experience. As Mississippi officials quickly learned following Gray's death, truth and reality are never quite as important as what people perceive to be true. Despite continuing attempts to convince the witnesses and the public that Jimmy Lee Gray died quickly and painlessly, the reports of the prisoner smashing his head furiously into an iron pipe continued to circulate.

Jimmy Lee Gray may indeed have been unconscious and unaware that his head was striking a metal pole, as prison officials vigorously asserted, but that no longer mattered. What mattered was the widely held belief that Gray had been made to suffer unnecessarily. In death, the despised child killer had found new friends who clamored for change. Many reasoned that even though executions might be necessary, they ought to be humane. Soon after the debacle of Gray's death, Mississippi officials installed a headrest on the chair to avoid similarly embarrassing situations in the future. A few months later, the state legislature adopted a bill that would eventually replace execution by gas with lethal injection. The bill was written so as to apply only to persons sentenced to death after July 1, 1984.

Concern for finding a more humane form of execution may have been high on the legislators' agenda, but so was their determination not to provide death row prisoners with new avenues of legal appeals. Legal experts in the legislature and in the attorney general's office feared that changing the actual method of execution after a person had already been sentenced would leave the state open to unnecessary legal challenges. Accordingly, the legislative and executive branches fashioned the law so that it applied only to persons condemned to death after the bill was signed into law by the governor. This action guaranteed the continued use of the gas chamber in Mississippi for at least another decade.

But the execution of Connie Evans was my responsibility on this night. Looking at my watch, I was taken by surprise because it was almost time to move from the last-night cell. Dropping to one knee, I nervously explained to Connie that a medical technician would come in very soon to attach electrodes to his chest for the cardiac monitor. There was a moment of awkward silence, suddenly broken by the sound of a key turning the lock on the heavy door. When it swung open, the tiny cell was inundated by the din of the execution room. Closing the door behind him, the male nurse entered and quietly went about his task. Otha Ferguson quickly attached the electrodes for monitoring heart activity to Connie's chest. I noticed that the prisoner's skin was not adorned by the homemade tattoos that inmates often sport.

When Otha left the room, I turned to tell my prisoner it was time to take the final walk. Before I could speak, however, Connie told the chaplain he wanted to pray. Ron Padgett extended his hand to Connie's, and then the forlorn-looking figure asked me to pray with them. We all stood, our hands joined while reciting the Lord's Prayer. I did not know whose hands were trembling the most—mine or those of the man about to die. When the chaplain finished leading us in prayer, Connie thanked him for his help; they said good-bye with a warm embrace. He next turned to me, and as we shook hands Connie thanked me for the many kindnesses extended to him by the staff. Then, with a sheepish laugh, he asked if the warden would be embarrassed if an inmate hugged him. Searching fruitlessly for comforting words, we silently embraced for a long moment.

With the appointed execution time of one minute past midnight just seconds away, I knocked on the metal door twice. The lock turned and the door swiftly swung open. Chaplain Padgett and I somberly escorted Connie Ray Evans the final few feet from the last-night cell to the execution chamber. Entering the room, the condemned man exchanged a few words with several of the officers, his voice still clear and natural. Two senior officers, Fred Childs and Barry Parker, led him into the chamber and eased him into the large black chair. There was nothing ordinary about this chair, I thought, as I watched Evans nervously sit down. Somewhat oversized, with a seat that was higher off the floor than usual, the chair seemed to swallow its occupant. Connie was of average height and slender in physique, but he was sturdy and muscular. Looking down, I noticed that his feet did not quite rest flush on the floor: Somehow it all made the chair seem much more gruesome. Otha Ferguson entered the chamber and rapidly connected the electrodes on Connie's chest to the wire leads extending from the cardiac monitor through the chamber wall. Immediately the machine began emitting a steady beeping sound.

I stood by silently, with the chaplain and Dwight Presley flanking me, as the officers secured Connie in the chair. I felt numbed, and for a second or two the officers appeared much the same. Huddled on either side of the chair, they at first seemed reluctant to complete their assigned tasks, but then they rapidly secured the leather straps about his arms, chest, and legs. Connie was wearing routine prison garb—a light blue short-sleeved shirt, white trousers with a blue stripe down the side, tennis shoes, and socks. Although prison policy called for men on death row to be executed in the red jumpsuits they routinely wore, I had granted his request to wear regular inmate clothing. It was a harmless wish that was of no significance to the state, but, since he raised the issue several times in his final days, it seemed important to him.

Next the officers swiftly immobilized Evans's head with the harness and chinstrap that protruded from the headrest. I silently prayed for a quick and painless death for my prisoner, and a process free of mechanical failure or human error for me. There were so many things that could go wrong. The very first occupant of Mississippi's gas chamber, a notorious killer named Gerald Gallago, was the victim of human error that required a half hour of furious repair work before the execution was carried out. The more recent Jimmy Lee Gray fiasco was very much in my mind when Dwight Presley whispered that he hoped the headrest would work. I tried not to dwell on the probing questions that would have to be answered should any part of the process misfire.

Despite being immobilized from head to toe, Connie Evans was visibly shaking. His face was etched in fear, and his large, dark brown eyes moved rapidly from side to side, trying to comprehend what was happening. The chaplain stepped into the chamber to exchange some last words with him. Feeling helpless and out of place, I marveled at the calm with which Connie had walked the steps taking him to his death. I surmised it involved acceptance of and resignation to one's fate, something like the feelings experienced by the terminally ill. I had reflected often on such a scenario, concluding that if I faced the executioner I would either slip into unconsciousness out of absolute terror, or have to be dragged, kicking and screaming, to my death.

Ron Padgett left the chamber, and Col. Fred Childs stepped back in. Evans looked up and asked him, in a voice that was tremulous and barely audible, "What should I do?" How terribly sad a question, I thought. Yet how many times had it been repeated by other pathetic figures? Placing his hand on Connie's arm, and responding in a voice that unmasked his compassion, Childs explained that as soon as the gas struck his face he should breath in deeply two or three times—then it would all be over.

When Childs and Barry Parker left the gas chamber, Connie asked how much longer we had to wait. Still lost in thought, I collected myself and gently recited the explanation I had offered earlier. I had to await a telephone call from the attorney general. He would either clear the way to proceed with the execution or notify me that a reprieve had been granted. It was a sobering explanation to be sure, but I wanted no secrets, no misunderstandings between us. Connie had a right to know everything that was going to happen, and I had a responsibility to be honest and forthright with him. At that late hour no one, least of all my prisoner, expected any legal relief. Although we both knew that courts had granted many last-minute stays of execution, Connie Ray Evans had run out of legal arguments. At a few minutes past midnight, after six years on Mississippi's death row, he would also run out of time.

Feeling frustrated, I turned and stepped out of the chamber, asking Chaplain Padgett to go back in and remain with Evans. While Ron conversed quietly with the condemned man, I found myself again pensively scanning the scene that was unfolding before me. Not moving my eyes from the condemned man and his pastor, and speaking to nobody in particular, I ordered the curtains screening the gas chamber to be opened. The telephone rang almost immediately in the witness room as Dwight Presley relayed my order (though not my anger) to Steve Puckett. Even before Presley hung up, the curtains opened quickly, and the witnesses started at the sight of the prisoner already strapped in the chair.

This room, filled to capacity, was a study in human types. There were nearly two dozen witnesses in all, including members of the press, law enforcement representatives, defense attorneys, state attorneys, and prison employees. Most were subdued, anxious to perform their chore and return to life as they had known it as quickly as possible. There were also those who seemed to regard the whole thing rather blithely. One of the media representatives, an obvious boor, made no secret of his excitement at having been selected for the panel. Seated next to him was a local law enforcement official who had expressed considerable anger and disappointment at not being included on the original list of witnesses. Prevailed upon by superiors to include the gentleman, I had reluctantly added one more curiosity seeker. I watched him, seated in the second row, as he indulged himself in the attention being showered on him by the reporter. I almost chuckled aloud as I pondered what a perfect match the two made. Among the remaining witnesses there was low, sporadic conversation as they waited expectantly.

Standing in front of the observation window that occupied the right side of the chamber, I haltingly held up two fingers for Connie to see, indicating it would be a few minutes yet before his life would be extinguished. Suddenly aware of feeling exhausted from the emotional roller coaster I had been on, I knew I would feel relieved when it was all over. Connie mouthed "Okay," letting me know that he understood my message. Then, much to my surprise, he flashed a little smile.

How long the final minutes would be for both of us! I turned to speak to one of the physicians, but I was interrupted by the shrill ring of the red telephone on the wall behind me. The sound came without warning, and it instantly drowned out all other noise in the room. Instinctively, I spun around to the observation window of the gas chamber. Our eyes met and locked in an embrace of fear and anticipation that only a warden and his condemned prisoner could understand. I felt paralyzed, helpless and unable to reassure him. His eyes were questioning, pleading as they searched for a flicker of hope in the incessant ringing of the telephone. For a second I thought I should say something to him, but what would it be? My head was reeling from the commotion around me, and my heart pounded with such fury that I knew everyone in the room could hear it. The sweat poured off Connie's forehead, and I noticed again the awful, suffocating heat.

The telephone was still ringing, but somehow it sounded far away. Feeling a tugging at my shoulder, I turned to see Dwight Presley motioning for me to take the phone from him. I stepped away, as if I could somehow postpone the inevitable by not answering. Finally, I took a deep breath and slowly lifted the phone to my ear; before I could utter a sound, however, it slipped from my sweaty hand to the floor. Embarrassed, I cursed the heat and reached for it again. My lips tightened and I struggled to speak. My eyes had not left the young man who was enduring endless anticipation as he sat waiting in the gas chamber. I nervously listened to the voice of Assistant Attorney General Sonny White informing me to proceed with the execution.

At last, on an oppressively hot, muggy July night in the flat emptiness that is the Mississippi Delta, the time had arrived to exact justice from Connie Ray Evans. Handing the telephone to someone behind me, I knew that I had nothing left to say to my prisoner. Our eyes had never strayed from each other, and my expression conveyed the message—there would be no reprieve this night. I slowly shook my head, and Connie closed his eyes. A lone tear streamed down his cheek.

Although this was to be my second execution in less than two months, there was no way I could have prepared myself for the difficult task of sending a young man whom I had grown to know and like to his death. In the nearly four years since our first meeting, I had concluded on numerous occasions that I would gladly swap Connie Ray Evans's date with the gas chamber with that of any one of dozens of other prisoners—not all of them on death row.

Looking around, I became aware of the uncharacteristic quiet that had settled on the room. The only noises were the drone of the pump that would discharge the deadly gas from the chamber and the constant beeping of the heart monitor. Technology had found its way to the execution room. A few years before, physicians merely checked the prisoner's heart with a stethoscope. When a heartbeat could no longer be detected, the prisoner was pronounced dead. Modern execution protocol required a more exact measurement of death.

I briefly looked at the monitor and was startled at the wild, erratic display on the screen. I asked the doctor if Evans would die of cardiac arrest before we could execute him. What a welcome relief that would be! I knew, though, that nothing, not even Providence, would dare to foil the state's right to kill Connie Ray Evans.

Staring blankly into the witness room, I felt dulled by the terrible reality that was now upon me. The witnesses, too, had been interrupted by the sudden ringing of the telephone in the execution room. They were waiting—waiting for my order to kill another human being. Stepping into the chamber, I felt the hair on the back of my neck stand up. Positioning myself directly in front of my prisoner, fumbling with the death warrant in shaking hands, I slowly began to read the document. In a quivering, staccato voice, I read for what seemed an eternity. Gazing into Connie's eyes, I stumbled through the closing chapter of this bizarre ritual, asking him if he wished to make a final public statement. His eyes welled with tears now, and I was struck by his childlike appearance. This was not the same cold-blooded murderer who had arrived on death row six years before. His tears were not just those of a young man fearful of what lay beyond death's door; I was convinced they were also tears of genuine sorrow and pain for the tragic hurt and sadness he had caused so many people.

How insane the whole process seemed! I knew this man, I believed his life was worth saving. I had argued so forcefully to the governor. Even though he was privately sympathetic, legally and politically there were no grounds that would allow him to justify commuting Connie's death sentence.

As I looked on, I thought if what Americans want from executions is vengeance and retribution, let them witness what I was about to do. I was not forgetting the victim of Connie's crime or his family. My heart ached for the wife who was made a widow, and for the children who were left fatherless, by a single act of greed and selfishness. Nor was I oblivious to the need for society to achieve justice. But I questioned how an execution would end the lifelong pain and suffering endured by the victim's family. Killing Connie Ray Evans would not bring his victim back from the grave. Perhaps it would afford some temporary measure of satisfaction to the widow and her children, but the hurt and pain would never be completely eradicated, not even by the execution of a lonely, frightened, and—yes—remorseful young man.

I knew there were those who would cheer wildly at the terror the man strapped in the black chair was feeling, and still it would not be enough. Look how his victim suffered, they would clamor; yet what I was watching convinced me that the execution itself must almost be a relief for the prisoner, for even before his lungs were filled with cyanide gas a full measure of retribution had already been extracted from Connie Ray Evans. I was not feeling sorry for him, or pitying him. Evans had committed a terrible crime, for which he needed to spend the rest of his natural life in prison. I could hear the chorus of angry voices rising in a crescendo of opposition again. Justice, let there be justice! A life for a life! Why should he live at taxpayers' expense, while his victim lies silently in a premature grave? After all, he denied another man the chance to share life together and grow old with his wife, to experience the joy and pride of watching his children grow up. He cheated an innocent man of his right to a full life.

Valid questions, I thought, questions that defy easy answers. But as I stood inches from a man I was about to execute, I did know one thing for certain: as a society we were supposed to be better than the Connie Ray Evanses of the world.

Try as I might, I was unable to tear my eyes from his. He gazed up at me, as if in shock. His eyes were wet, with a glassy appearance that conveyed a chilling acceptance of his impending death. Connie spoke quietly, haltingly. He wanted to whisper his final words to me privately, he said, and I leaned down so I could hear him. He thanked me for being his friend. I started to speak, but he asked me to wait, and then told me softly, "From one Christian to another, I love you." I wanted to respond, but no words would come. Now I was the one in shock, shaken to my very soul. We had talked so much in the final weeks and days, our conversations always relaxed and easy; yet now, when it seemed most important, I was at a complete loss for words. What does one say to a man who has told his executioner that he loves him? The question hurtled through my mind, seeking answers that were not there. In the weeks since the most recent execution, I had slept with troubled dreams, fitfully trying to make sense of the whole thing. Looking at the man in front of me, I wondered if I would ever sleep peacefully again. I reached down and placed my hand on Connie's arm, gently squeezing for what seemed a very long time. As I stood up and prepared to leave him, for some mysterious reason I felt as if all my tensions had dissipated. The fear inside me released its icy grip, and I knew that I would fulfill my responsibilities. Connie had indeed forgiven me.

Quickly turning around and stepping out of the chamber, I ordered it sealed, even while realizing that some of my self remained inside. There is a part of the warden that dies with his prisoner. Nobody else can suffer the intimacy of impending death, or experience the pitiable helplessness involved, in the same way as the warden and his condemned prisoner. Both are victims, unwilling captives of a human tragedy that is presented on a stage shrouded by mystery. It is played before a small, invited audience that is hidden from public view. Acted out in the darkness of night, as if to shield the citizenry from the awful reality of it all, an execution is a drama that panders to public fear and to a lust for vengeance, which is otherwise disguised as justice.

Executions strip away the veneer of life for both warden and prisoner. Connie Ray Evans and I transcended our environment, and the roles in which we had been cast. The two of us had somehow managed to become real people to each other. There were no more titles or social barriers behind which either of us could hide—I was no longer a prison warden, and he had become someone other than a condemned prisoner. We were just two ordinary human beings caught up in a vortex of events that neither of us could control.

Prepared to speak the fateful words that would achieve retribution for all Mississippians that night, I was deluged with one last onslaught of doubt. As warden of the Mississippi State Penitentiary, I understood my duties and responsibilities better than anyone. Twenty years in corrections had hardened me to many of the woes that emanated from daily prison routine. One does not, I conceded, run a maximum security prison for a living without encountering difficult decisions every day. I certainly knew, better than most, that those who run prisons must rule with their heads, not their hearts. Such an outlook sounds cold and cruel, but I entertained memories of everything from simple fistfights to riots, hostage takings, and brutal murders. The realities of prison life simply did not allow room for common sense to be overruled by emotion.

There was a certain philosophy I had developed regarding the entire issue of capital punishment. My personal feelings were not germane to any part of the process. I had a job to do; I did not look forward to carrying out an execution; I tried to handle the situation as just another part of the job. I had often witnessed the cold, unfeeling violence of inmates, and over time my senses became numbed by it. I presumptuously concluded that I was both prepared and well suited for playing the role of executioner.

Nothing, however, could prepare me for what I saw and felt when I supervised my first execution. There is nothing commonplace about walking a healthy young man to a room, strapping him into a chair, and coldly, methodically killing him. I knew after the first one that if it ever did become routine, if I found myself no longer haunted by doubt, then I would know the time had come for me to leave corrections behind.

Oh yes, there was the matter of who actually pulled the lever to drop the cyanide crystals into the sulfuric acid. Mississippi paid an executioner five hundred dollars to perform that function. But I discovered that my hand was on the lever as well. The executioner could not, would not, proceed until I gave the order. Regardless of who performed which function, the hand of death reached out and touched each of us in that execution room. Try as I might, I could not separate myself from the horribleness of it all.

The moment had arrived and could be delayed no longer. I looked into the chamber, my attention again focused on the chair. An old inmate who had escaped its clutches years before, when his death sentence was commuted, once referred to it as the "black death." How appropriate a name, I thought. My eyes shifted quickly to the lever. The executioner's hand was gripping it firmly, ready to drop its deadly cargo. I stood there, worried about what my wife and children and my friends would think of me. But most of all, I wondered if my God would forgive me.

Prepared to utter the words that would execute Connie Ray Evans, I looked into his eyes, drawn by the need for one last glimpse of him alive. Our eyes met for the final time. How, I asked aloud, had we traveled such different paths, only to be brought together in the dark confines of Mississippi's death row. "How in the hell did you and I get here?" I knew then that I had come full circle.

Titicut Street

We must proceed . . . in the belief that every human being
has a spark somewhere hidden in him. . . .
If we accept the idea that each human, however "bad,"
is a child of God, we must look for that spark.

John Conrad, University of California

As a rookie at the Massachusetts Correctional Institution in Bridge-water, the last thing on my mind was that I might one day be required to execute another human being. Besides, at that early stage in my career, I was not at all certain that working in corrections was how I wanted to spend the rest of my life. The prison business was still relatively new to me, since I had worked at Bridgewater less than a year. In that time, however, I had already seen enough to convince me that the penitentiary concept, as originally envisioned by Quaker reformers more than two centuries ago, was largely a failure—an archaic relic that neither responded to the needs of the inmates nor effectively protected the public it was sworn to serve.

Reflecting on twenty-five years in the business, I am still not sure what motivated me to make a career of it. In spite of my early conclusion that the present system is largely a failure, I was undaunted. Once introduced to corrections, it did not take long for me to discard any notion I had of attending law school. The system had seized my interest like a powerful narcotic.

What began innocently enough as a college internship soon became the first step to a career. I arrived home from Viet Nam in the summer of 1969 and almost immediately returned to Northeastern University in Boston, where I had attended school before enlisting in the air force. Although I did not do particularly well academically, I ranked high in athletics and fraternity parties. Four and a half years of active military duty had been a maturing experience. Upon my return, I enrolled in a new undergraduate program in criminal justice. At the time, I was flirting with the idea of entering law school and then possibly pursuing a political career, so I thought a degree in this field would be the perfect prelude.

During the late 1960s antiwar hysteria prevailed, especially on the nation's college campuses, and Northeastern University was no exception. The civil rights movement was at its zenith, as a wave of liberal social reform swept the land. America was a nation at war with itself, calling into question long-cherished beliefs and institutions. The criminal justice system came under public scrutiny and criticism as never before. A new era was emerging in which even the most staunch defenders of the status quo acknowledged major flaws in the nation's ailing justice system. A growing chorus increasingly called for sweeping change, demanding better-trained and better-educated police, increased support for a penal system that put rehabilitation on an equal footing with punishment, and a judicial system that was truly blind when dispensing justice. It was an exciting time, and it afforded me a rare opportunity: the chance to be part of a period of change, to become an active participant rather than an interested spectator.

As autumn wore on, my academic advisor informed me of a possible job (actually, a student internship) at the Massachusetts Correctional Institution in Bridgewater. Since I wanted practical experience doing something, anything, in the criminal justice field, my response was enthusiastic.

When the day of my interview arrived, I arose earlier than usual, filled with anticipation. The morning was overcast, with a November wind that had been howling most of the night. It was a little early in the winter for Massachusetts to be getting its first blast of Canadian air; yet, when I bounded down the stairs to breakfast, skipping every two or three, there was Don Kent, Boston's venerable television meteorologist, predicting falling temperatures with a hint of early snow flurries. I found the prospect of snow three weeks before Thanksgiving exhilarating. After spending my hitch in the air force stationed in places like Alabama, Texas, and Viet Nam, it had been a while since I had seen any white stuff, and I was looking forward to it.

Nervously, I finished dressing, all the while reminding myself that it was just an interview—no guarantees, no promises. I wanted the job badly, however, and was determined that nothing would prevent me from getting it. My mind raced, assailed with doubt one minute, filled with confidence and determination the next. My father, ever the skeptic, had admonished me about Massachusetts politics. He meant that I would have to "know someone" to get the position, yet I knew no one, at least not in a political sense. Truthfully, it was not a political job, but my father remained unconvinced. As far as he was concerned, if it was a state job it was political, and therefore probably beyond my grasp. Dad's views about government and politicians, especially of the Massachusetts variety, were legendary within our family. I could not restrain a hearty laugh as I thought about his words of encouragement the night before.

Fortunately, I did not have far to drive. Despite having grown up in the Massachusetts south shore town of Easton, just twenty minutes from Bridgewater, I had never before laid eyes on the prison. Located some thirty-five miles south of Boston, it was situated on approximately twelve hundred acres of land on the southernmost edge of the town of Bridgewater. A sleepy New England community that proudly traces its origins to Captain Myles Standish and the fabled Native American Sachem Massasoit, Bridgewater's economy depended largely on two state-owned enterprises, the prison and a teacher's college. The community boasted of being home to the first normal school established in the United States, Bridgewater State Teacher's College. The prison, on the other hand, was often mentioned in less glowing terms.

Traveling Route 28 south toward Cape Cod, I saw no hint of a prison save for a small wooden sign marking an otherwise obscure entrance. It read MCI Bridgewater and had a small red arrow that directed me to a narrow, winding paved road. Quickly leading into a heavily wooded marsh, the road meandered into deeper woods, adding to the shroud of mystery that surrounded "the farm," as many locals still called the prison. First opened in 1854 as an almshouse, in its early decades the institution consisted merely of a few wooden buildings; these were destroyed by a fire set by an inmate. The prison was quickly reconstructed and remained known as the State Farm. The title was retained until the 1950s, when it was redesignated the Massachusetts Correctional Institution at Bridgewater.

While I continued to navigate the entrance road, I realized that even though I had never seen the place it was not totally unfamiliar to me. Occasionally, some crisis or infamous personality who was incarcerated there would thrust the prison onto the front page of local papers. Without doubt, this obscure institution housed some of the most dangerous prisoners in the commonwealth: Albert DeSalvo, the alleged Boston Strangler who had single-handedly terrorized that city; the less well known but no less infamous Olsen, vicious murderer of two young boys in Brockton. They and many others were confined within the walls of the section of the prison designated the State Hospital for the Criminally Insane. Residents of the surrounding communities generally never paid much attention to the prison. But inmates like DeSalvo and Olsen invariably brought unwanted attention and publicity. DeSalvo rocked people in southeastern Massachusetts when he managed to escape. Although he was recaptured uneventfully a few days later, his short return to freedom served to remind those living near the facility of the uncertainties of life in a so-called prison town.

Olsen's presence in Bridgewater, and the publicity attendant to his case, had especially aroused the local populace. Two young boys from the nearby community of Stoughton were enjoying a family outing at a popular recreational area in the local city of Brockton. Olsen stalked the Logan brothers through the park; after brutally assaulting and murdering them, he burned their bodies and buried them in shallow graves.

The prison had also received unwanted attention in the 1960s with the release of the documentary film *Titicut Follies*, a name the director, Frederick Wiseman, borrowed from its yearly inmate amateur show. The film offered a revealing glimpse of life inside Bridgewater, but it also generated immediate controversy and was eventually banned from public screening in Massachusetts by the state supreme court. Although the justices ruled that the film violated the inmates' right to privacy, what it really did was to expose the substandard conditions in the prison.

I could not help wondering about DeSalvo and Olsen, as well as the hundreds of other inmates confined within the prison's walls. What became of such men in places like Bridgewater? Did their looks, physical characteristics, or mannerisms belie their true personalities? Could one sense, just by observing them or listening to them, the evil that lay within? Was there any rational explanation for the pain and suffering unleashed on innocent, unsuspecting victims like the Logan brothers by predators such as Olsen?

My thoughts were suddenly interrupted as the winding road left the dense woods behind and, without warning, entered open pasture. At last I was able to catch my first glimpse of this most infamous of Massachusetts prisons. Still distant, but now clearly visible, it stood atop a subtle rise. Clusters of rooftops peeked over the prison walls, great mounds of concrete that rose twenty feet in the air. Approaching from the rear, I could see redbrick towers overshadowing the prison landscape, looking down imposingly on the inmates. The structures seemed intent on keeping the outside world at bay, perhaps even more than on keeping the prisoners securely confined within. Upon seeing the institution, I was filled at once with excitement and foreboding— it looked every bit the maximum security prison I had imagined. All at once, the entrance road abruptly ended, intersecting with Titicut Street, which ran in front of the prison's main entrance. I drove into the visitors' parking lot and for a few moments could only sit and stare in awe. If I had entertained any doubts about wanting the job, they were quickly dispelled by what lay before me just yards away. I did not know then, anymore than I do a quarter of a century later, what fascinated and intrigued me about the place, but it was something I sensed immediately.

Striding briskly across the street toward the main entrance, I noticed that the menacing gray clouds indeed held promise of the predicted snow flurries and that an increasingly sharp wind made it feel even colder than it was. Looking about at the elms and maples that lined Titicut Street, trees that seemed lifeless-looking in the face of approaching winter, I was struck by how much their bare appearance resembled the huge concrete and redbrick prison. Trees devoid of foliage for the winter ahead, grass long since turned brown from October frosts, the Canadian air that gripped the scene—all accentuated the sense of stark coldness that prevailed everywhere I looked.

Approaching the entrance, I quickly whispered a silent prayer for a successful interview. Pushing the heavy wooden door open, I was grateful to feel the warmth of the entranceway. A glass-enclosed room, fortified with steel bars, was nearby; an officer inside directed me to sign the visitors' log. I quickly produced identification and announced the purpose of my visit as another officer appeared in the entranceway and informed me that I would be searched. Since it seemed a logical enough thing for a prison to do, I endured my first frisk search with as much aplomb and dignity as I could muster. After escorting me through an electronically controlled door to a flight of stairs leading to the administration building, the officer directed me to a small waiting room, tersely instructing me to remain there.

The letter from the institution's personnel office informed me that the job for which I was interviewing was a counselor position in the Alcohol and Drug Addiction Treatment Center. I was to be interviewed by John Metevier, the director of the prison's Department of Social Services, so I was a little surprised when two men entered the waiting room to greet me. A rotund but distinguished-looking gentleman introduced himself immediately as John Metevier. Speaking with a deep, resonant voice, his firm handshake pumping rapidly, he radiated a warmth and enthusiasm that quickly put me at ease. I tried to restrain my smiling gaze, amused that Metevier's pencil-thin mustache and impeccably combed-back hair reminded me of the television comic Jackie Gleason's character Reggie Van Gleason. The other man, whom I took to be the personnel officer, was quite different in appearance from Metevier. Short and wiry, he wore his salt-and-pepper hair in a 1950s crewcut and sported gold-rimmed glasses that accentuated his thin, sharp facial features. He was dressed in a starched white shirt, and a very thin bow tie, and puffed on a pipe, with wisps of aromatic smoke constantly swirling around him. As we shook hands, I noticed that his grip was considerably less spontaneous, without the enthusiasm of Metevier's. But, looking down, I saw why—his hands were gnarled, the joints full of protruding knots, probably from arthritis. Nor were the palms of his hands smooth, as one would expect of someone bound to a desk; rather, they were rough and callused. When he finally spoke, his voice had a nasal quality that I had not expected. Removing the pipe from his mouth, he introduced himself as Charles Gaughan, warden of the institution.

Trying to hide my surprise, I could only hope my face did not betray the instant anxiety and discomfort I felt at the prospect of being interviewed by the warden. Although uncertain, even as I examined him unobtrusively, what the head of a prison should look like, Charles Gaughan was not what I had envisioned. He seemed to be a holdover from another age. At first glance, he did not impress me with the "command presence" I was expecting of a person in his position. That notion was rapidly dispelled, however, as Gaughan demonstrated his obvious abilities as a take-charge individual. He controlled the interview, asking very direct questions, probing my interest in corrections, my career goals, even inquiring about family plans. Metevier was largely an observer, and following a couple of perfunctory questions he quickly deferred to Gaughan again. The warden concluded the interview by offering me the job. It had all taken less than twenty minutes, but in that time I realized that Charles Gaughan was an astute individual who was probably well suited for his role as chief executive of a large penal institution. As I would later discover, his quiet demeanor masked a tenacity that aided him in surviving the rough-and-tumble politics of the Massachusetts prison bureaucracy.

Those first three years of working at Bridgewater were not especially remarkable. I was just one more returning Viet Nam veteran, trying to put the pieces back together so I could get on with my life. The opportunity to work at the prison was an important step in that direction. There would be many practical lessons along the way, but it was Charlie Gaughan who had the most profound and lasting impact. For whatever reason, he took me under his stewardship, relishing the role of mentor; and, in me, he found an eager and willing protégé.

After I had worked at Bridgewater for several months, it was at Gaughan's suggestion that I transferred to the security staff as a full-time correctional officer. I had thoroughly enjoyed my few months as a counselor, and was grateful for having worked under John Metevier's tutelage. He was a good supervisor, one who became a trusted friend as well, but I looked forward to new and different experiences as a correctional officer. The warden considered it important that I experience the harshness of the "real" prison world, as he called it—the world of the guard and the convict.

Within a few days I entered a shadowy, often sinister environment that few people outside prison walls ever fully comprehend. Gaughan had warned me of difficulties to come. He told me that when I ceased being a counselor and put on a uniform I would be treated differently, not only by the inmates but also by my former colleagues in the counseling ranks. He knew what he was talking about! Many of the inmates reacted with scorn and contempt, while some of my erstwhile fellow counselors seemed to become detached and indifferent.

It is a rite of passage in corrections that rookies are assigned to the midnight shift, and I was no exception. In Massachusetts, duties for first-year guards also had much to do with seniority and union rules. I learned early that in almost every issue that concerned officers seniority would prevail, even if it was a detriment to prison operations.

My first night at work moved slowly. The duties were routine, with the monotony broken only by the hourly counting of inmates and an occasional encounter with the shift supervisor as he made his rounds through the prison. It was not exactly what I had in mind, but I had to start somewhere.

Gradually I found my niche in the security staff. Correctional officers are, by nature, suspicious characters who do not make close friends easily. Eventually I won acceptance and respect from most of them, and life within the walls seemed just a bit more tolerable. My tenure as one of the boys was short-lived, however. One night about a year after joining the correctional officer ranks, I was assigned to the prison infirmary; this was pretty quiet work, since most of the inmates housed there were elderly.

My primary duty was to make hourly rounds among the rows of beds in the large open ward on the second floor, calling in the inmate count to the prison control center. The senior officer remained on the first floor, drinking coffee with the infirmary night nurse. A man in his thirties, the supervisor was a corrections veteran who had "earned" his easy assignment by virtue of seniority. The sum of his physical activity usually consisted of locating a mirror, removing a comb from his back pocket, and carefully grooming his shiny, black mane so that it was slicked back just so. His swagger was noticeably more pronounced once his hair was again in place.

The nurse was a frumpy, overweight, middle-aged woman with dishwater blond hair and a constant emphysema-like wheeze and cough who was never seen without a cigarette dangling from her mouth or fingers. Her face, leathery and ruddy, occasionally was covered with tiny, broken blue blood vessels; thick long nails and fingers were stained deep amber from constant contact with nicotine. She begrudgingly made her rounds only when medicines were to be given.

One night, an inmate was restless and agitated, continuously crying out in his sleep. The man, who spent most of his time in a fetal position, was at least in his seventies and was literally alone—the drab, depressing infirmary was the extent of his world. Incarcerated in Bridgewater for more than forty years, he had not received a visit in recent memory, since his family had died off or simply lost contact with him. The shell of a person that lay in the 1930s-style white-enameled hospital bed was a statistical casualty of a bygone era. Committed to Bridgewater as an alcoholic vagrant, he had somehow fallen through the bureaucratic cracks. Although he could have been released years earlier, he had no place to go and no one to go to, so the prison had long since become his home.

The man's mind had left him years before; much of the time, he thought he was a cat. Sadly, some officers taunted the old man by making loud meowing sounds, to which he would respond in kind. On this night, though, he awoke from his fitful sleep and began making his catlike noises spontaneously. After a few minutes the senior officer and the nurse came up the stairs and entered the ward. By then, some of the other inmates were stirring. One patient started meowing back, and soon the whole room sounded like a menagerie. Assuming the nurse was going to sedate him, I approached the inmate's bed with the senior officer, who directed me to restrain the old man's arms. As I did, he slapped the inmate about the face and head several times in rapid succession, without warning or provocation. Shouting and cursing while hitting him, the officer told the old man that if he didn't shut up he would kill him. The nurse also began cursing the inmate and then asked me if I wanted "a piece of him."

The old man was nothing more than an unknowing intrusion into the nightly coffee-drinking routine of the nurse and the officer. Satisfied that they had taught him a lesson, the two calmly turned and walked back downstairs. Trailing after them, I could feel my face flushed with anger. Unwisely, I grabbed the senior officer by the arm, demanding to know what justification he had for striking the inmate. He jerked away from my hand and angrily retorted that I should keep my mouth shut, reminding me that since I had held the old man down I was just as guilty as he was.

I turned and stalked off, listening to the inmate cry out in pain, which intensified my anger. Wracked by guilt, I spent the rest of the night debating what, if anything, to do. No stranger to violence in the prison, I had been required to use force on unruly inmates on any number of occasions, but this had been different. There was no marauding convict directing violent rage and physical harm against inmates or staff—there was only a pathetic-looking, unsuspecting old man whose mind was totally gone.

Somehow, it was the nurse who bothered me most. Not exactly the picture of compassion that one often associates with her profession, she was an embittered, hateful person who found delight in mistreating prisoners. She was, however, smart enough not to personally abuse an inmate, at least to my knowledge.

That morning I decided to report the incident to Charlie Gaughan. Foolishly ignoring the prison's established chain of command, I took advantage of my friendship with the warden. Believing that I was doing the right thing made reporting the incident no easier, however—I remained torn between what I believed to be right and loyalty to a fellow officer. Much to my surprise, I did not feel a whole lot better after discussing the incident with Gaughan. I was, in fact, assailed by considerable doubt, for his reception was not what I had expected. He seemed lukewarm at best, and gave the impression of being more concerned with protocol than substance. His first question was whether I had followed the chain of command, and if not, why not. I was being put on the defensive and could not understand why.

In the end, the officer was disciplined and transferred to another assignment; the nurse was allowed to remain. At times, it seemed as though I was the one being punished. No longer very popular with my colleagues, on occasion I would receive harassing phone calls at my duty post, while at other times officers would request not to be assigned to work with me. Usually I was just given the silent treatment. I had violated a cardinal rule of prison staff—not to snitch on another employee. Though I did not realize it at the time, Gaughan had taught me my first valuable lesson in the workings of prison bureaucracy. By their very nature, prisons must function with a high degree of organization and thrive on a systematic, disciplined approach. Most of them are also very much semi-military, emphasizing the chain of command and resolving problems at the lowest level possible. From Charlie Gaughan's perch, I had cheated my supervisors of the opportunity to address a problem. It was a lesson that I failed to grasp at the time. Little did I know that the other officers' attitudes, as well as the warden's chilly reaction, would actually prepare me for far more severe confrontations with brutality at the Mississippi State Penitentiary.

In spite of the incident with the old inmate, and in the face of overwhelming odds, Charlie Gaughan still ran a good institution. The prison was old and in deplorable disrepair—the cells, for example, had no sinks or toilets, only a bunk and a chamber pot. The legislature paid scant attention to the institution's deficiencies, except to criticize Gaughan after some major problem came to light. The correctional officers, while granting the warden their begrudging respect, seemed to fight him a great deal, although much of their criticism seemed part of normal labor union rhetoric. They perceived him as too inmate oriented (a charge, I would discover, that is very popular among correctional officers). Unquestionably, in Gaughan's view, his first responsibility was for the welfare of the inmates placed in his custody, not for that of the officers.

Charlie Gaughan was no more able to satisfy all the inmates, however, than he could the officers and staff. Such is a warden's life. Prisoners occasionally express their wrath in very personal ways. In one memorable incident, Gaughan denied a kitchen worker a Christmas furlough. The disgruntled inmate vented his anger on everyone who ate lunch in the staff dining room the next day, just a few days before Christmas. The man was working on the serving line, smiling eagerly and extending heartfelt holiday greetings to one and all. Heaping generous portions of spaghetti onto our plates, he encouraged us to come back for seconds. Knowing he had been turned down for a furlough, I was most impressed with his attitude, convinced he had handled the setback quite well. As a Sicilian American with a fine appreciation for Italian food, I fully indulged myself—going back not once, but twice more. Prison food is not home cooking, but my love for spaghetti simply overcame common sense. I left the dining hall with my hunger satisfied completely.

In the next twenty-four hours many employees were struck with a nasty intestinal virus, or so it was thought. Since my wife, Miriam, whom I had met and married in the air force, was still in Texas completing her two-year tour of duty as an air force nurse, I had made plans to fly to San Antonio to be with her for Christmas. My "virus" attacked with unforgiving vengeance at thirty-five thousand feet. The flight attendants were most understanding, arranging a seating change that placed me in the closest proximity possible to the lavatories. More than slightly amused, they even placed one of the lavatories on permanent "occupied" status so I would not have to wait in line. To say the least, I endured an uncomfortable trip, since the lavatory is where I spent most of the six-hour flight from Boston to San Antonio. It turned out to be a most memorable Christmas.

I returned to work a week later and discovered the real cause of the "virus." The angry inmate had poured laundry detergent into the pot of boiling spaghetti, assuredly exacting revenge not only on Charlie Gaughan but on everyone else unfortunate enough to have enjoyed the privilege of dining with him that day. The warden, however, had the final word. The inmate's smiling face disappeared from the staff dining hall, never to be seen in those parts again!

After three years in the Massachusetts prison system, my career took me to Mississippi; later assignments would follow in Florida, Missouri, and Mississippi again. No matter where my travels took me, I never stayed out of touch with Charlie Gaughan for very long. A brilliant administrator, he survived the heat of Massachusetts politics with his integrity and reputation as a superb professional intact. The wiry little man with the Harvard education continued to have a profound impact on my career, advising me on matters large and small whenever I felt the need for his counsel. At a time when the Massachusetts Department of Corrections stood tall, with such indisputable leaders as John Gavin and John Fitzpatrick, Charlie Gaughan struck an imposing figure as a principal among them. Later, when the commonwealth's penal system became a holding area for a succession of inept, politically motivated appointees, Gaughan continued to represent stability, continuity, and professionalism. His shadow loomed larger than ever, the epitome of what had once been right and good with the business of corrections in Massachusetts.

During my novice years at Bridgewater, Connie Ray Evans was a mere boy. I could not know that I was embarking on a journey that would ultimately change me forever. By the spring of 1972 I had received my degree and decided to move my family to Mississippi. One thousand miles away, a skinny, unremarkable twelve year old was beginning his adolescence. Still possessing the innocence of childhood, there were no noticeable warning signals, no hint yet in his life of the calamity that awaited his victim and him in just a few short years.

As I walked out of Bridgewater for the final time, Connie Ray Evans and I were about to move closer in our unsuspecting journeys. A new chapter was waiting to unfold for me at the Mississippi State Penitentiary. Before summer's end in 1972, I would catch my first glimpse of the state's death row. Though separated still, Connie Evans and I would one day be hurled into a climactic encounter inside Mississippi's execution chamber.

Rude Awakening

This is a kind of funny thing for a warden to say,
but Tiny and I were friends. . . .
Because we're all just human.

Bill Armontrout, Warden, Missouri State Penitentiary, 1989

In the Massachusetts prison system of the early 1970s, the word "execution" was rarely mentioned. It was not taboo—it just was not an issue. A generation had passed since the last occupants of the electric chair had been dispatched to oblivion. Sitting in stony silence since the late 1940s, the chair had suffered from a lack of public support, as well as from a succession of anti–death penalty governors. The nation had been under a self-imposed moratorium on executions for several years, with the last one having occurred in 1964. Furthermore, most public opinion polls in the early 1970s revealed a populace that was increasingly opposed to using the death penalty. So, by the spring of 1972, there appeared to be little likelihood that I would ever have to confront the issue firsthand, especially if I chose to remain in Massachusetts.

Ultimately, however, I elected to leave the familiar environs of Massachusetts. Just after my graduation from Northeastern University (where I received a bachelor of science degree in criminal justice in June 1972), my wife and I packed our one-year-old son and our belongings, and struck out for Mississippi. Massachusetts was home, and the decision to leave family and friends was not easy, but I had a job awaiting me at the Mississippi State Penitentiary, more popularly known as Parchman. It appeared to be a good opportunity, and the deputy warden who had extended the offer was enthusiastic about my prospects for rapid advancement.

I had become familiar with Parchman quite by chance, first learning about it in an article by the University of Mississippi sociologist Columbus Hopper. By happy coincidence, my wife's parents lived just a couple of miles from the campus in Oxford, so I decided during one of our vacations there to contact Professor Hopper, hoping to learn more about the penitentiary. Our first meeting, in 1971, proved most beneficial, as he not only provided me with valuable information about Parchman but also graciously arranged a tour for me. I would eventually visit the prison several more times over the next year, thoroughly intrigued by what I found.

My very first sighting of Parchman was memorable, so different was it from any prison I had worked in or read about. It did not fit the stereotype of a penitentiary. My wife and I set out from her parents' home early one spring morning in 1971, the prison just a ninety-minute drive away. As we drove leisurely west on Highway 6, the picturesque and hilly north Mississippi landscape disappeared without warning as we entered the sleepy town of Batesville. Suddenly, before us stretched the easternmost rim of the vast flatland known as the Mississippi Delta. Dotted with occasional swampy, snake-infested cypress groves, fields of cotton and soybeans stretched to the horizon. It was a stark contrast to the gently rolling countryside we had just left behind. Every few miles a magnificent plantation home, shaded by stately pecan trees and magnolias, would rise up from the lush fields. Within view of these mansion-like structures were the "shotgun shacks" that housed the sharecroppers who worked the planters' land while living in abject poverty. It was indeed a world of immense contrasts.

After what seemed considerably more than the eighty miles indicated by the map, we approached a sign directing us to Parchman, seven miles down Highway 49 south. The endless expanses of cotton and soybean fields all looked the same, with the neutral color of the dirt broken solely by the stark whiteness of the unpicked cotton. Only the farmers could have known where one's land ended and another's began. We knew Parchman was nearby, however, after passing a highway sign that read: Penitentiary Area Next Two Miles: Do Not Pick Up

Hitchhikers. Off to the right, a long row of houses came into view, along with clusters of redbrick buildings. Slowing down, we encountered another sign that announced the entrance to the Mississippi State Penitentiary. Turning right off the highway, I stopped at a guard shack, where an officer logged us in and obligingly provided directions to the administration building.

Miriam and I were greeted by a well-dressed, distinguished-looking gentleman named Jack Byars, one of the associate wardens. Of average height and a somewhat slender frame, Byars had a fair complexion that was dotted with freckles. His stack of wavy, almost reddish, hair was combed back except for a small part on one side. When he spoke, his voice belied his Mississippi roots. His career in the army, and his many years away from home, had partially obscured his native accent. Returning home after retiring from the military, he was brought to Parchman by Tom Cook, who was then warden. His combination of administrative experience and political savvy allowed him to navigate his way through the ranks of the prison bureaucracy quickly, and Cook soon made Byars his associate warden.

Jack Byars possessed a relaxed demeanor, and his engaging personality quickly put us at ease. (In truth, my wife was considerably more at ease than I was, hitting it off with him almost immediately.) Ushering us into his office, he inquired as to where we were from. Simultaneously, I replied "Massachusetts" and Miriam said "Mississippi." We both laughed nervously, and Byars chortled as he told me that he knew from my accent that I was no Mississippian. As the associate warden leaned back in his richly appointed leather chair, all the while staring intently at me, his eyes resembled narrow slits. Resting his chin on fingertips that were brought together as in prayer, he maintained his steady gaze. He seemed to have become suspicious the second I blurted out that I was a Yankee from Massachusetts. I shifted uncomfortably in my chair and cleared my throat several times. Attributing most of my anxiety to an overactive imagination, I found myself, nevertheless, more distressed each time he repeated "Massachusetts, huh." After he repeated it for about the fourth time (he pronounced it "Massatoosets"), I thought I should attempt to engage in some kind of dialogue with him, though what I really wanted to do was to correct his pronunciation! Nodding my head assertively, I forced a half smile and said, "Yes, Massachusetts."

I turned to my wife, who was always good at sending me non-verbal cues in such situations. I could not believe that "Yes, Massachusetts" was all that had come out. Obviously, neither could she—her expression seemed to tell me, "Way to go, Don." Although trying to convince myself that I had no reason to be leery of this man, my worst fears were confirmed in the next instant. Raising one of his bushy eyebrows, Byars asked, with a trace of a smile, "What brings somebody from Massatoosets all the way to Parchman, Mississippi?" After laughing nonsensically, and babbling that my home state was indeed a long way from Parchman, I was again at a loss for something to say. Sensing my continued unease, Miriam came to my rescue. Ever the epitome of the genteel Southern lady, she flashed her vivacious smile and politely directed Byars's attention to her roots in Mississippi. The associate warden's entire demeanor appeared to undergo a complete transformation. He no longer seemed suspicious or distrustful, and his gaze finally left me, much to my relief, to focus on Miriam instead. She was totally at ease as they covered their Mississippi ancestry, at least as far back as the Civil War.

Actually, the entire meeting could have been a social disaster, but Miriam saved the day with her calm manner and finest Southern charm. Not surprisingly, I became merely an interested bystander as Byars and my wife swapped old Mississippi tales and entertained each other thoroughly. At the moment that the associate warden leaned back in his chair and offered her a cup of coffee, I knew everything was going to be okay, with the exception of the prison coffee supply. Miriam was capable of draining a coffee pot faster than Juan Valdez could pick the beans. Only an unwitting stranger like Byars, naïve about my wife's excesses, would let her near the coffee supply.

Some forty-five minutes later, the associate warden summoned an officer to escort us on a tour of the penitentiary. We exchanged pleasantries as we left, and Byars invited us to join him and some other prison officials for lunch at the warden's guest house. I quickly accepted the invitation, for I had developed a ravenous appetite while listening to Byars and Miriam swap family and military stories.

Once we were outside the administration building, it quickly became evident that Parchman was no ordinary prison. There were no tiers or cellblocks, no twenty-foot walls or gun towers—there were not even any fences. Missing were the license-tag plants, furniture factories, woodworking shops, and metal-fabricating sheds that I had become accustomed to in Massachusetts. The Mississippi prison, rather, was a sprawling complex of more than twenty thousand acres of fertile Delta farmland, where the emphasis was on raising crops and putting inmates to work in the fields. It was a throwback to another time and place.

Inmate work crews were everywhere as we traveled the main road that bisected the penitentiary. Referred to by our tour guide as "guard row," the road was lined on both sides with identical wood-frame houses, by and large drab and in various states of disrepair. Mostly built in the 1930s under the Work Projects Administration, the houses were provided to prison employees for a nominal rent of ten or twenty dollars a month. Because of Parchman's isolation, the state over the years had deemed it necessary to provide housing for prison employees. Such an approach ensured an adequate presence of staff for immediate response to emergencies like escapes or inmate disturbances. Frequently, several generations of one family would continue to live and work at the penitentiary.

Our journey down guard row soon brought us to a gravel road. The escort stopped in front of a wooden sign with the paint peeling off; its faded red letters proclaimed Camp 16—MSU. The maximum security unit (MSU) was the only inmate housing area at Parchman that resembled the more traditional kind of penitentiary I was familiar with. Double fences topped with concertina wire surrounded the small building. Gun towers anchored the four corners of the fence line, and a double-gate sallyport prevented anyone from entering the unit without notice. I could not help wondering about the men who were confined there. The officer solemnly pointed out that the unit was called "Little Alcatraz" by staff and inmates alike because of its reputation for holding death row prisoners and the penitentiary's most recalcitrant inmates.

Entering the sallyport, we were cleared momentarily to view the gas chamber, which was separated from the back tier of death row only by the so-called last-night room. Although I had not asked to look at the chamber, I was curious about it. I had seen the Massachusetts electric chair, but I had no conception of what a gas chamber looked like.

Stepping out of the car, the officer unlocked an exterior metal door that opened directly into the execution room. Peering through the doorway, I was immediately awed by the sight of the chamber. The heavy metal door to the chamber itself was open, revealing the steel chair into which the condemned prisoner was strapped. I was moved, as if by some unseen force, to step inside the chamber and touch the chair. I wondered about the men who had faced death in this object—who they were, what they were like, why their lives ended inside a hideous-looking contraption filled with lethal gas. Our guide invited me to occupy the chair, explaining that many of those who toured the prison wanted to experience sitting in it. How odd some people are, I thought, that they should be so attracted by the macabre. I politely declined the offer.

The death chamber was filled with ghosts, the spirits of mankind's most hideous nightmares. I shuddered at the thought of the terrible struggles and horrific events that had taken place there. The officer, however, asserted that working on death row was "just a job." When I asked if he had ever witnessed or participated in an execution, he said no but made it quite clear that he would if presented the "opportunity." He then complained at length about the infrequent use of the gas chamber, which Mississippi had last used in 1964, seven years earlier. I casually remarked that it was apparent that capital punishment had fallen into disrepute with both a majority of the public and the courts and that the United States had probably seen the last of executions. I had no idea how wrong I was, and how intimately familiar I would eventually become with the dark world inside "Little Alcatraz." Nor could I then appreciate the naïveté with which I dismissed the death penalty as a relic of a bygone era in America's justice system. As we rode away from the camp, I turned for a final look. Though we had not entered the cellblocks inside, I imagined them to be not very different from those of Massachusetts. Envisioning the faceless men who were confined inside the building that was fading from view, my thoughts returned to the gas chamber. Fate, though still in the distant future, lay in wait; barely more than a two-hour drive away. Fate also awaited Connie Ray Evans. Though we were still worlds apart, the trip to Parchman had brought us closer, our paths destined for an apocalyptic encounter sixteen years later. On that last day, I would stare into the eyes of a soft-spoken man of twenty-six and ask myself what could have gone so wrong. But on a sunny spring afternoon in 1971, Connie Ray Evans and I were still just unknowing innocents.

In that era, Parchman was Mississippi's only penitentiary. About two thousand men, and fewer than a hundred women, were incarcerated there, housed in a series of small "camps" that were scattered across the more than twenty thousand acres that lay within the facility's borders. The sheer magnitude of the place was difficult to comprehend on first viewing. It was not a prison that officers patrolled on foot, prowling tiers of cellblocks or sweatshop-style prison industries. "Patrolling" Parchman meant traveling on horseback among the vast network of agricultural plantings that crisscrossed the land; riding from the front entrance of the prison to the gateshack at the rear required one to cover a distance of six miles!

Each of the eighteen or so camps had a particular function. A few were specialized, such as the "disability camp," where inmates operated the prison laundry, or the "front camp," which housed inmates who worked in the administration building as clerks, janitors, and maintenance personnel. Parchman's primary emphasis, however, was on farming. Each of the "work camps" had a quota of acreage to maintain, and the inmates stayed very busy planting, hoeing, harvesting, cleaning, and processing everything required for sustenance. The prisoners raised vegetables, beef, poultry, and pork; tended a dairy herd that provided milk, butter, and cream; and operated a slaughterhouse and canning plant. But in 1971, though the crop was in decline, cotton was still king at Parchman—thousands of acres were planted, contributing a substantial amount of cash to the state coffers.

Everywhere we looked, there were large groups of inmates working the fields under the watchful eyes of armed men on horses. The officer guiding us said the groups were called "long lines." Prisoners were taken from the camps to work in the fields; if there were a hun-

Inmates unload vegetables harvested from Parchman's vast fields.

dred men they were spread a hundred rows across (thus the terminology), with two armed guards on horseback in front of the line and two behind it. The lines trudged from one end of a field to the other, back and forth all day in a monotonous routine that rarely ceased. Inmates were required to work from 6:00 A.M. until 6:00 P.M., with an occasional water break, as well as twenty minutes for lunch. The officer slowed down to give us a closer look at the men toiling in the fields just a few dozen yards away. It was an impressive sight, and the system was not without its positive points.

In some respects, Parchman was a penologist's dream. Instead of two thousand prisoners crammed into crowded cells within four walls, the Mississippi State Penitentiary scattered them in small units that usually housed no more than a hundred to two hundred men. This certainly made it difficult for large numbers of inmates to engineer disturbances of any major consequence.

A second advantage was the labor-intensive nature of the work programs. While some of the farming was mechanized, most of it relied on inmate labor. All the vegetables were picked by hand, as was the cotton. It was a backbreaking job under a broiling sun, but it provided enough work to keep inmates occupied most of the time, except for the winter months from mid-November to mid-February. Idleness was a major problem in most prisons, since there never seemed to be

Inmates unload hand-picked cotton at Parchman in 1986.

enough work to occupy all the inmates. For example, most prison jobs in Massachusetts—making license tags or highway signs—were mechanized and not very labor-intensive. But twenty thousand acres of land could produce almost limitless possibilities for work! The only constraints at Parchman were occasional bad weather and the short winter months.

Finally, another more subtle, but no less important, advantage seemed to influence the relatively tranquil environment at Parchman—most of the inmates worked outside. Surely, I thought, there must be some benefit to serving time in a penitentiary that does not confine a man for endless hours each and every day inside a cramped, dark cell.

As we began the return trip to the administration building, our escorting officer casually mentioned the "shooter" system. When I asked him for an explanation, what I heard, and then saw, astounded me. The men on horseback—whom I had been able to view only from a distance as they guarded long-line inmates in the fields—were inmates themselves! The shooters were "trusties," or trusted convicts, who had been given guns with which to guard other prisoners. The officer laughed when he saw the surprise on my face, remarking good-naturedly that obviously convicts were not permitted to have guns in Massachusetts. I would discover later that using inmates as guards was not unique to Parchman, most other states in the South having employed the system at one time or another. It apparently worked quite well, as there were seldom any disciplinary problems among the shooters. The institution relied heavily on the use of trusties for everything from guarding other inmates to running the prison's telephone system. The officer explained that fewer than seventy-five civilians (including support, administrative, and medical staff) were employed at Parchman. Most tasks, including guarding inmates, were performed by other prisoners who had demonstrated trustworthiness and ability.

By the time we pulled up to the guest house for lunch, I had been thoroughly captivated by what I had seen. As we entered, Miriam and I were again met by Jack Byars, who introduced us to about a dozen other prison officials and guests. A very tall, powerfully built gentleman strolled across the room to greet us. The handshake of John Allen Collier, who had only recently been appointed warden by the governor, had a vigor that would have been the envy of most politicians. Ruggedly handsome, Collier possessed the healthy outdoorsman's complexion of the gentleman farmer that he was. Once we were seated, he introduced Miriam and me to a man who was already being served by white-coated inmate waiters. Nearly as tall as Collier, he was much more slender, with a narrow face accentuated by slightly reddish cheeks and a rather long, pointed nose. His hair showed signs of graying in places. He spoke in a deep tone, with a decidedly Southern accent. Senator Corbett Lee Patridge, who had grown up within a stone's throw of Parchman, knew more about the penitentiary than almost any other member of the legislature. His importance to the prison administration was enhanced by his chairmanship of the Mississippi Senate's Corrections Committee.

As lunch progressed, it became painfully obvious that the ebullient Patridge was accustomed to making speeches and holding court. He did not let so small a matter as a meal interfere with his speechifying. The powerful senator only barely disguised the true meaning of his politically inspired diatribe. He meant to put Warden Collier on notice that he would have to get along with him if he entertained any hope of a successful term. Judging from Collier's comments and general demeanor, he got the point.

Miriam and I left Parchman that day impressed with what appeared to be a remarkably industrious institution. Without a doubt, the facility had its share of problems; just like any other prison—there were serious deficiencies that had been ignored by a succession of legislatures and governors. Even as we visited that first time, however, the forces of change were slowly beginning to gather momentum. Within the year, they would alter the institution forever.

By the time I visited Parchman again, in March 1972, a storm of legal controversy had enveloped it. An obscure, illiterate inmate named Nazareth Gates had filed a lawsuit against the State of Mississippi, charging it with running a prison that violated the U.S. Constitution. Except for Tom Graf, the prison administrators did not seem to take the lawsuit seriously. Even when the U.S. Justice Department joined the suit on behalf of the inmates, the attitude of prison officials was largely to ignore it as a nuisance.

Such a viewpoint was not totally unfounded. Historically, federal courts had taken a hands-off approach to inmate litigation. They were hesitant to become involved in the administration of prisons, which was the province of prison officials. The corrections administrators in Mississippi had no reason to believe that the Gates lawsuit would be treated any differently. If the federal court ruled in favor of the inmates, it would place itself squarely in the position of usurping the state's authority to run Parchman as it deemed necessary. Still, there was a strong hint of change to come—just across the river, a federal judge in Arkansas had already declared that state's penal system to be in violation of the most basic of constitutional standards.

The legal controversy swirling about Parchman in the spring of 1972 was not lost on one deputy warden, however. The only administrator who had any formal training in penology, his voice nonetheless remained a whisper in the wilderness. Accused by colleagues of shouting that the sky was falling, he was unable to convince them that the Gates case was a threat to be taken seriously. He offered me a job as a case manager, or inmate counselor, a position new to the institution. If I accepted, I would help establish a classification system, a formal method of determining inmate housing placements, job assignments, educational needs, and mental health status. It was hard to believe that any prison of the 1970s lacked the essentials of a proper classification system, but Parchman had been neglected for so long that it still operated under a philosophy from the 1940s. The silver lining was that becoming a case manager presented me with a chance for a job with tremendous responsibility and good potential for career development. I eagerly agreed to report for work on the fifteenth of June.

My last three months at Northeastern University were the most difficult, because I was so eager to start my new job. But graduation day finally neared, and I made one last telephone call to confirm arrangements with Parchman. I spoke with the deputy warden who had offered me the job. No last-minute glitches—everything was ready to go. The following morning, my family and I began the trek to Mississippi.

Our arrival at Parchman was welcome, if only because of the twenty-two-hour drive. Although weary, I was eager to meet with the deputy warden and get settled in quickly. (The moving van was due to arrive with our furniture within a few days.) But a funny thing happened on the way to the penitentiary—I lost the job! Strolling into the suite of offices that housed the warden and the deputy wardens, I confidently announced myself in an "I'm here" approach. I was somewhat disappointed to draw a blank stare from the secretary. When she responded with an amused "You're who?" I sensed there might be a problem. Moments later, my worst fears were confirmed. I told her that I was there to see the deputy warden who had offered me the job. Well, much as it pained her, she felt obliged to inform me that he was no longer employed there. His last day had been Friday! Frantically, I explained to the nice lady that I had just spoken to him Thursday and that he never mentioned that he was leaving. After another amused half-smile, she blithely explained that he did not know he was leaving until Friday. Since his abrupt departure had been involuntary, the deputy warden had failed to mention to anyone that he had offered me a job, with an agreed-upon salary and a fine three-bedroom brick home thrown in for good measure. Even if he had told anyone, the secretary assured me, no one would have listened.

That Monday morning seemed a rather ominous beginning, to say the least. Obligingly, the secretary had me wait while she discussed the matter with someone who could help me. Help me, I thought! I vacated an apartment in Massachusetts, packed up my family, hired a moving company, and drove twelve hundred miles to a new job, only to find out that the guy who promised me the job was himself no longer employed! I sat in the waiting room, fidgeting with my fingers. Then a familiar figure strolled in, extending his hand in greeting. Jack Byars remembered me!

As we settled in his office, Byars apologized for any misunderstanding. Oh, there was no misunderstanding, I protested, unless it was on the part of the penitentiary. I interviewed for a job, the man offered me a job, and now I was there ready to begin work. Byars again apologized profusely, but explained that the deputy warden in question had never discussed this with anyone. Since he had been terminated, it was unlikely that the prison could fulfill a commitment he was not authorized to make in the first place. But, Byars went on, in the interest of fairness, and because Parchman was always interested in hiring "bright, young help," the penitentiary would certainly find a place for me in the organization. As I sat there intently listening in disbelief, a smile became frozen on my face, the kind of smile that can quickly evaporate into tears. Parchman would provide me with housing, though of a sort perhaps not quite as nice as I had been promised. I would be put to work on the security staff, since neither Byars nor anyone else in the administration had any knowledge of a case manager's position ever having existed. As he patted me on the back and ushered me out of his office, Byars smiled and assured me he would do everything possible to make my decision to come to Parchman a positive one. Be in his office the next morning at eight o'clock. With those fateful words of encouragement, I began what would be a brief but hectic year at Parchman.

The next morning I was camped on the deputy warden's doorstep at seven-thirty. Jack Byars entered the administration building involved in an animated discussion with a thirtyish man in uniform; he had reddish brown hair, and freckles marked his face. Byars approached, greeting me and quickly introducing Danny K. Thomas, chief of security for the penitentiary. I was impressed that someone so young had risen so far. A few moments later, the youthful-looking man came out of Byars's office and, flashing a wide grin, welcomed me on board. He told me to call if I needed his help in any way. Only later would I discover just how difficult even a simple telephone call could be!

Before long, Byars came bounding out and asked me to join him in the warden's office. John Allen Collier, whom my wife and I had met and talked with over lunch just a few months before, loomed large even when seated behind a desk. Without getting up, he displayed his boyish grin, assuring me all the while that he was delighted I had decided to come to work at Parchman. Byars had obviously discussed my predicament with Collier, as the warden quickly offered a perfunctory explanation regarding the recent departure of the other deputy warden. In the process, he asked me to spell out the agreement that I understood I had regarding employment at the penitentiary. While I quickly explained it for the umpteenth time, Collier's eyes kept shifting rapidly from me to Byars.

After still another profuse apology, the warden explained that, of course, there was nothing he could do: the deputy warden had offered me a job that did not exist; even if it had, it would not have been filled without approval from the warden. I was again beginning to feel slightly insecure. Warden Collier continued to assure me that there was a position in the security ranks that would make good use of my experience and education in corrections. Well, I thought, it was not what I had been promised, but at least the administrators recognized my abilities and education. At that point I had no choice but to accept whatever they offered. A moving van full of furniture was due to arrive in the next few days, and I had no place to unload it!

After a little more discussion, I left Collier's office feeling that everything was about to work itself out. Quickly convincing myself to make the best of a rather disappointing situation, I declared myself ready to meet new challenges. As we walked the few feet back to Byars's office, Jack announced that he was going to assign me to work at the First Offender's Unit, under the direction of Sergeant Tom Bennett. Byars pushed the "inflate here" ego button a little, pronouncing me the ideal type of young officer to work with youthful offenders.

Bennett was waiting outside Byars's office. The deputy warden quickly explained to Bennett that I was hiring in that day and would be working with him for a while. The sergeant smiled as we shook hands, and he assured Jack Byars that he would take care of me. Although pronouncing myself fit to meet whatever challenges Parchman held in store, I would soon encounter things that were included in no textbook that I had ever read.

A man of average height and slender build, Tom Bennett had a fair complexion and a head of thick black hair. He seemed friendly enough at first. I was something of a curiosity to him; in truth, I probably had him wondering what stroke of misfortune had caused him to be stuck with a rookie from Massachusetts. As we walked to his pickup truck, he informed me that we would first stop by the personnel office and get me signed up on the payroll.

Prisons, like law enforcement agencies, operate in such a way that not everyone is cut out for them. Many employees wash out in the prison environment; this does not necessarily imply their ineptitude—

working in a prison is just not for everyone. After three years of experience in the Massachusetts prison system, however, I was not remotely concerned about whether I would make the grade at Parchman—not concerned, that is, until I entered the private world of the prison's personnel office. As we walked through the door, Bennett chuckled, remarking that we were about to step into the public relations office. It was a private joke, one that I did not understand at the moment, but I would soon discover the thrust of Tom Bennett's humor.

The large woman seated at the desk just inside the door visibly resented our sudden intrusion on her turf. Looking up, she focused her scowl on Bennett, who slowly stammered an indifferent greeting. She returned it with a gruff "What?" My companion attempted to explain our reason for interrupting her routine. She replied rudely, "They always send new people over here at the wrong time." Although Bennett invoked the deputy warden's name several times to assure her of the legitimacy of the interruption, the lady was clearly unimpressed. After considerably more complaining, the woman finally consented to process me in. Moments later, as I prepared to leave, I thanked her profusely for "extending the welcome mat." Teeth clenched, the woman managed to rise to her feet, casting a large shadow as she did so, and graciously acknowledged my thanks with a grunt. Bennett and I both beat a hasty retreat, content to go fight inmates all day! Now I understood the humor in Tom's earlier reference to "public relations."

I would eventually find Tom Bennett to be a quiet, soft-spoken individual, possessed of a quick wit and good sense of humor. On that first day, however, he was full of questions about my experiences in Massachusetts, what its prisons were like, and what the convicts did for work. I do not recall that he ever addressed me by my first name, calling me "Yank" instead, which he had decided was a good name for me.

We slowly rounded a ninety-degree curve in the dusty gravel road, bringing the camp into view. On the right was a large fenced-in area full of turkeys. Adjacent to the turkey pen was a dilapidated house that looked like it had not been occupied for a very long time. That would be my home, Bennett said. Noting the disappointment in my face, he assured me somewhat sardonically that I would get used to it. Across the road, nestled behind more dwellings, were three poultry houses, each about a hundred yards long. Bennett laughed as he pointed them out, telling me what I could already sense, that the neighborhood severely tested the olfactory senses. I had a sinking feeling as I looked around, wondering what I had done to my family. I had not even been on the job for a whole day and was already having serious doubts.

When I strolled alongside Bennett into the camp for the first time, however, I felt better. Even though I knew I had much to learn, in there, surrounded by convicts and barbed-wire fences, I was in my element. The gun-toting shooter who opened the gate for us was called Pappy, a reference to his early fiftyish age. Not only had Pappy been to Parchman before but he had been a shooter there for as long as he could remember. The First Offender's Camp he helped run was not physically impressive. A one-story redbrick building constructed in the late 1960s, it was the newest camp at Parchman. Enclosed by a single fence, it was monitored by two gun towers situated in opposite corners and by a front gateshack. The camp was built entirely with inmate labor—even the bricks were made at the penitentiary.

Prisons have a grapevine that rivals the communication network of Ma Bell. It did not take long for word to spread that the camp had a new officer. To the inmates I was a source of curiosity, a new "fish," just as a new convict would be. The next few weeks would prove to be interesting for both the inmates and me. No matter how seasoned or experienced a correctional officer is, he or she can count on being tested by inmates, particularly when taking on a new assignment. Tom Bennett introduced me to his cadre of trusties—kitchen workers, shooters, canteen workers, and cage bosses—the inmates who made the camp operate efficiently. The shooters and cage bosses were greatly despised by the other prisoners, and with ample justification.

Just grappling with terminology was a challenge. While all prisons utilize so-called trusties to one extent or another, the idea of letting one group of convicts carry weapons and guard other convicts would strike most corrections officials as preposterous. It had apparently worked effectively in Mississippi, though, as such a system had been in place at Parchman as long as anyone could remember. Trusties represented something quite different in the prisons I had been exposed to in Massachusetts. Those institutions employed inmate canteen workers just as Parchman did, with one notable difference: prisoners in Massachusetts were not permitted to possess currency. Convicts in Mississippi were legally entitled to have a maximum of twenty dollars in their possession (although many of them carried a great deal more). The money was supposed to be used to buy legitimate canteen items like cigarettes, soda pop, and candy. More often than not, however, the money was used to traffic drugs or finance prison prostitution and other inmate rackets. That Parchman convicts could possess currency was just one revelation that would astound me in the coming months.

The inmate operators of the penitentiary's canteen garnered a great deal of power. On a routine day such a trusty might handle hundreds of dollars in cash; on a good day he handled thousands. As in most settings, money in a penitentiary means power, and Parchman's canteen operators had plenty of both. Most of the inmates did not mess with the canteen man very much—they knew he was the sergeant's "hip boy," personally selected to handle such a sensitive position and under his sponsor's personal protection. There was money to be made in the canteen as well, and camp sergeants and their canteen operators often skimmed profits to line their own pockets. Considering that in the early 1970s the starting pay for an officer was three hundred dollars a month, it was little wonder that camp sergeants felt free to subsidize their paychecks illegally. And then there were the cagebosses. They were an entirely new breed to me, one that would require further explanation. Bennett responded to my query by matter-of-factly stating that cagebosses were among the toughest cons in the camp. They had to be, for they were expected to maintain order in the dormitory cages, particularly at night.

Stepping through the door into the camp, we entered a large open area with tables and chairs, obviously the inmate dining room. To the left of the entrance was a walled-in area about the size of a large office, which served as the canteen. On both sides of the dining area were inmate dormitories, referred to as "cages." To the left of the dining hall was the "gunmen" cage, and on the opposite side was the trusty cage. "Gunmen" were inmates who did not hold some kind of trusty status. They wore blue denim trousers with a white stripe down the leg, while trusties wore white denim trousers with a blue stripe.

I had not worked in any Massachusetts prisons that were constructed in dormitory style; single cells were preferred by prison officials in Massachusetts and other parts of the country. As one might expect, single cells are much more expensive to build than dormitories, but they are thought to be safer for both inmates and staff. I was amazed, then, as I looked at the two cages. There were rows of beds in each, separated only by homemade partitions, some of wood, others as simple as flattened cardboard boxes.

The First Offender's Camp had the smell of a prison, difficult to describe but unmistakable. Perhaps mildew blended with a generous portion of institutional antiseptic sums it up best. (Prison floors mopped daily with heavy solutions of chemicals give the casual observer at least the odor of cleanliness.) The convicts stared impassively, though there were only a few faces. Most of the beds were empty, their occupants out in the fields hoeing cotton. A few wandered up to the bars, wanting a close look at the newest intrusion into their drab routine. After showing me the kitchen and trusty quarters, Bennett bypassed the gunmen cage and ushered me outside. We were on our way to inspect the house my family and I would live in. It was just a few yards from the camp, but already the heat of the day had us both sweating profusely.

"You're the new driver," Bennett said matter-of-factly. We slowly walked down the gravel road to the house, while I awaited an explanation. "What's that?" I finally asked. The sergeant grinned like a schoolboy who had just played a trick on the new student. "I don't suppose they have drivers up there in New York or wherever it is you come from . . ."

"Massachusetts," I interrupted, somewhat sarcastically. Bennett had not forgotten where I was from; he just did not want to say the name because he could not pronounce it correctly. No matter how careful he was, it always came out "Massa-too-setts." In fact, I had not yet talked to anyone at Parchman who knew how to say it.

"Yeah, well, I knew it was from up there somewhere," Bennett responded with a chuckle.

"So," I asked, "just what do you mean I'm the new driver?"

"Well, a driver is the fellah that runs the long line out in the fields. The driver gets the work done, whatever it might be, whether it's planting vegetables, hoeing cotton, or picking cotton. He's the guy that supervises the inmates and ensures they get the assigned work completed."

Never was there a more apt piece of terminology. The driver, always referred to by the inmates as "Cap'n," drove the long lines furiously. From six o'clock in the morning until six o'clock in the evening, the long lines worked under the broiling sun, often at a blistering pace.

Bennett inquired about my knowledge of horses, presuming that there were not many jobs in Massachusetts prisons that required riding skills. Pride and a lack of common sense clouded my response. Somewhat flippantly, I advised my supervisor that Massachusetts did indeed have horses and that I was an accomplished rider. Registering a mixture of surprise and prankishness, the sergeant informed me my experience would come in handy, inasmuch as the drivers rode horseback all day. I suddenly became queasy. Having failed to mention that my vast experience in horsemanship was limited to riding the merry-go-round at Nantasket Beach's Paragon Amusement Park, I tried to conceal my sudden uneasiness from Bennett, but I was not sure that he was convinced. Anyway, I confided to myself, just how difficult could riding a horse be? If he (or she or it—whatever a horse is called) did not do right, I calculated, I would simply blame it on the animal's reluctance to follow instructions from a stranger.

By the time Tom Bennett had finished describing my duties, we were cutting across the front yard of my new home. "Convenient," I remarked unenthusiastically. Trying to make the best of a depressing scene, I played up my enthusiasm about being able to walk to work in a couple of minutes. As we approached the steps leading to the front door, I marveled at the sight that stood before me. Actually, the first thing that caught my attention was the smell—after all, there were a hundred turkeys living twenty-five feet from my front door. They were also rather noisy, our presence resulting in prolonged calling among them. Bennett averred that I would get used to the smell, the heat, and the dust; pretty soon I would not even know the turkeys were there. Something told me he was engaging in a bit of understatement. But do not feel too unkindly toward them, he said with a mischievous laugh—after all, come Christmastime the penitentiary would give me a turkey. This made me feel a whole lot better about sharing my front yard with them.

Although walking, I was still turned to look at the turkeys when the sergeant grabbed my shoulder, shouting for me to watch out. The first of the three wooden steps leading to the front porch of the house was rotted out. Reaching for the screen door, he had to pull on it several times before it finally opened with a flourish, only to hang cockeyed on the bottom hinge. Assuring me that the house was basically sound, Bennett said that although it had not been lived in for a while a thorough cleaning and a few minor repairs would put it in good shape. That sounded reasonable to me, and since our furniture was not due to arrive for another few days there would be time to clean and paint the inside and to make some repairs. Maybe it would not be so bad after all, I thought, as we stepped into the living room.

I caught a glimpse of the first one out of the corner of my eye. Be calm, I thought, it was merely imagination, not a rapidly moving shadow silently disappearing into a gaping hole in the plaster wall. But then my worst suspicions were confirmed; I froze in my tracks, feet paralyzed in the doorway. My brain was frantically transmitting messages to my legs and feet to move, but they were not receiving the signals. As Tom Bennett suddenly hollered and stomped his foot on the hardwood floor, a dozen mice squealed and scurried in every direction, including one who, in an apparent state of confusion or wanton bravery, ran toward me. Although I was frozen in the door, it was not my wish to do anything that might discourage the rodent's departure. The creature moved rapidly on, and I became increasingly panic-stricken. What to do, I wondered. Suddenly, about halfway across the floor, the mouse stopped to take in the situation. By now, he appeared to be considerably larger than I had at first thought, at least the size of a wood rat. This was no ordinary creature. Then he moved closer, bigger now than a house cat. Bennett stomped again in an attempt to send him on his way, but to no avail. Then it happened—suddenly, without warning, the creature reared and with a loud, chilling squeak leaped right at us. I had no quarrel with the mouse—I merely wanted him to vacate the premises, especially if I was going to have to live there. Bennett, on the other hand, took unkindly to the rodent's apparent assault and brought the full force of his boot down on the beast with a shout. Needless to say, the animal's injuries were mortal. Curiously, not only did Bennett succeed in killing the thing but he made it look much smaller in death than it had appeared to me in life.

I should not let the mice bother me, he observed. When a house is not occupied, the sergeant dryly remarked, they get to thinking they can claim ownership. But they did bother me. Just as the movie character Indiana Jones has a mortal fear of snakes, so it is with me and mice. Having dispatched the rodent, Tom enthusiastically encouraged me to follow him on a tour of the rest of the house. My legs and feet finally, albeit unwillingly, began to move. As we sauntered through the two bedrooms and past the bathroom, a few more of the finest specimens of Parchman field mice retreated to the safety of holes in the walls and floors. Surprisingly, we did not see any in the kitchen, though they had left a convincing trail of evidence in various cabinets and drawers.

As Sergeant Bennett turned around slowly, his face lit up like a Christmas tree, and Tom asked if mice bothered me. Never considering for a moment that he had, moments before, seen the blood drain from my face, I shook my head negatively and assertively. If he believed that, he believed I was an expert in horsemanship too! How could I expect my wife and son to live in such a mess, I wondered. She was terrified of mice; the place had no air conditioning; there was no telephone (only those holding the rank of sergeant or above had phones); the dust and dirt were everywhere. I kept thinking about the comfortable apartment we had left behind in Massachusetts.

The tour of my luxurious new living quarters complete, Bennett told me to report for work at 5:30 the following morning. I climbed into my car to begin the drive back to my in-laws' home in Oxford, wondering how I could learn to ride a horse before the next day dawned. Perhaps my father-in-law, a lifelong farmer well experienced in the handling and management of animals, could provide some advice.

Later that evening, as I explained my predicament, he threw his head back in a hearty laugh that shook his large but gentle frame. His wife hurt my pride the most, however. Trying her best to restrain the laughter that threatened to consume her, my mother-in-law asked if I had ever even seen a real live horse. As my wife joined her parents in the cascade of infectious laughter, my humiliation was complete. Despite my strenuous protestations of past personal contact with "real live horses," neither my in-laws nor my wife seemed any more convinced than Tom Bennett had been earlier in the day. Obviously, I would face the next day totally on my own.

Morning comes early at Parchman, especially in the summer. The sun rises, casting a fiery glow across the morning sky as it begins to scorch the landscape. Elsewhere in the rural Deep South, when you take the first few breaths of a new day a burning sensation from crop chemicals strikes your nose, shaking you from the final throes of slumber. But in the Mississippi Delta it is the noise that first jars you awake. There is a particular sound to The Delta, the vast farming region that stretches from Vicksburg north to Memphis. It is not the early morning warbling of birds, or the chorus of insects and amphibians that announces the evening hours. The Delta sound—man-made, but no less noticeable than nature's—is the drone of a nearby crop duster, distant at first, but increasingly noisy as it swoops over a nearby field. At the first light of dawn, the masters of these machines begin their aerial acrobatics, smothering the local landscape with insecticides, fungicides, herbicides, and any other agricultural "cide" known to man. Sounding and looking like World War I fighter pilots, these aerial daredevils, at considerable risk to themselves, dispense chemicals to endless fields of cotton, soybeans, and rice on their way to market.

By the time I walked nervously into camp the next morning at 5:30, the inmates had been up for nearly an hour. The last few stragglers were finishing breakfast amidst much shouting from an older-looking man dressed in a correctional officer's uniform. Tom Bennett stepped from his office to greet me with a warm handshake and a friendly smile. The man who was shouting instructions to the inmates was the night watchman, the sergeant informed me. (Parchman did not operate in the eight-hour shifts routine in most prisons; officers worked twelve-hour shifts, except for Saturdays, when they labored half a day.) Bennett invited me to step outside with him. He told me that the trusty shooters would get the inmates formed into lines in a few moments and then introduce me to them. Did I have any questions, anything I was not certain of? I looked him square in the eye and said I was nervous as hell—everything was different from the prisons I had worked in. He assured me he would come out to the field and check on things frequently during the day. When I asked how I would know where to take the inmates and what to have them do, Tom just laughed and said to leave all that to the shooters. Then he put his hand on my shoulder and quietly told me that I did not have to ride a horse if I chose not to. But I assured him that I did have to, just like any other driver. I had to do things Parchman's way. What I did not know I would have to learn, and learn quickly, to have any credibility with inmates or staff.

Bennett steered our conversation back to the night watchman. He had been employed at Parchman for a number of years and had, at one time or another, worked in just about every camp. In the sergeant's view, the old man was a no-nonsense individual, perhaps a little on the "crazy" side. Although he was ill-tempered and did not seem to like convicts, he did his job, and that was all that mattered. Bennett suggested I try to get along with the old man, since my house would be next to his. Just then, the door of the camp burst open as inmates came piling out in what seemed like an endless stream. Tied to their belts they carried plastic cups, discarded plastic coffee jars, or anything else made of plastic that would hold water. Many wore bandannas, ragged towels, or other items of cloth around their heads to help ward off the heat and absorb perspiration; all wore baseball-style caps. As two of the shooters entered the camp's outside gate, five horses trailing behind them, another shooter was hollering at the inmates to get lined up quickly. Shambling past Bennett and me, several inmates exchanged greetings with us, but most simply gave a glancing nod of the head, uninterested in talking with their keepers.

The inmates quickly counted off while the shooters performed a head count of their own. There were a hundred and ten going to the fields. I was already sweating, and I was wondering what it would be like in the midday sun. When the count was complete, a youngish looking shooter hollered "a hundred ten on the line, Cap'n," and with that Bennett acknowledged the count for me. Then he motioned behind me with his head to a horse he had instructed the shooters to select for me, assuring me with his usual grin that the stud was perfectly safe. My first moment of truth at Parchman had arrived. As I turned around, the boyish looking shooter who had called out the inmate count was leading the horse to me. Buckling a .38 revolver around my waist, I grabbed the saddle horn and pushed myself up onto the horse with a sense of ease that surprised even me. Then Tom Bennett shouted for the inmates to give him their attention and, without fanfare, he introduced me as the new driver. It was time to go to work. As the line began to move in two columns down the gravel road to a distant field of cotton, I wondered about starting and stopping my mount, but such fears were unfounded. By habit, the horse followed along behind the last inmates in the line. My first day at work was off to a tranquil beginning. Plodding along atop the white quarter horse, I

An inmate work crew picks vegetables at the Mississippi State Penitentiary under the watchful eye of an armed officer on horseback.

tried to carry an air of confident experience with me. The sight of more than a hundred inmates quietly marching down the gravel road with hoes slung over their shoulders was impressive. It was a far cry from Massachusetts, where prisoners belonged to a union and "citizen-observers" were permitted in the cellblocks to spy on correctional officers.

On that first morning I had a lot of questions. I had been told by Sergeant Bennett that the inmates would be "chopping cotton" all day, in fact, probably all week. I had no idea what chopping cotton meant (it involves removing every single weed from around every single plant), but who better to ask than an inmate? So as I watched the line in front of me amble down the gravel road, I hollered to Steve, the boyish shooter who had done the count. I did not know it then, but Steve would turn out to be a true friend. He patiently taught me the secrets of Parchman's operation, what to watch for, which inmates to observe carefully. He also trained me in everything from chopping cotton to the delicate art of picking okra.

In the early days and weeks everything seemed foreign, but I quickly became acclimated to my new environment. Gradually gaining confidence and becoming more assertive, I was able to project the credibility that is so crucial to the success of any correctional officer's relationship with inmates. There were, inevitably, the tests that are a part of being a new employee. The first real confrontation occurred one day about midmorning as the long line was hoeing its way across a large field of cotton. One of the shooters casually announced that we had a "rabbit in the row." Thanks to Steve, my lead shooter, I had become familiar with most of the colorful vernacular that Parchman's vocabulary comprised. Without hesitation, I shouted to the shooters to stop the line and hold their positions. The keen-eyed trusties had, during one of their frequent counts, found the line to be short one man. None of the inmates had bolted, which would have been foolhardy, nor had any managed to sneak past the shooters, or so we thought. Such an occurrence was not impossible, however. Cotton grows rapidly during the summer, attaining enough height so that a man lying between two rows can go undetected. Inmates would occasionally attempt to crawl past the constantly roving shooters, hoping to reach some distant ditch at the end of the field. Most escape attempts were spontaneous and, in consequence, failed quite miserably. The number of attempted escapes, however, was rather high, sometimes as many as several dozen a year. This was not terribly surprising, though, since most inmates worked in the fields or lived in unfenced camps. Even when a prisoner managed to navigate his way past the shooters, however, he still had to confront the considerable task of getting off penitentiary land. Parchman's twenty thousand acres easily confused many a frightened inmate, causing him to run for hours, even days, without ever leaving the property.

The line had stopped, and the shooters ordered the inmates to remain motionless and perfectly quiet. The nearest ditch was still a good hundred yards away, which made it highly unlikely that the "rabbit" had managed to sneak past the shooters. It would have been easiest to allow the trusties to flush him out, but I could not do that. This was the first convict to test me out in the fields, and it was important that I handle the matter personally. The shooters, as well as the long-line inmates, were watching, and Tom Bennett had to know that I was capable of dealing with such situations on my own. When one of the shooters asked if I wanted Bennett notified, I snapped a rather ill-tempered no and ordered him to hand me his rifle. Sooner or later, the missing inmate would have to move again. He might just decide to scrap his short-lived attempt at freedom and suddenly jump up with hands in the air. More than likely, I thought, he would choose to remain hidden, hoping against hope that the unlikely would happen and that he would somehow find his way to freedom. In that event he would have to start crawling again, which would prove to be his downfall. I slowly moved my horse down the field a short distance, at the same time ordering the long line to move back several yards. It was like a game of cat and mouse, and the next move was his. I was certain that everything was working to my advantage. He knew that, too. Boxed in by gun-toting convicts who would not hesitate to shoot him on sight, he was lying among the rows in a stand of cotton that seemed to have no end, the sun beating down on him unmercifully. He had only one possible advantage: I was untested in an environment that was still new and strange to me. Oh, I had worked in other prisons, all right, and thought I knew convicts, but I had never been exposed to anything quite like Parchman, nor did I know its convicts. Their vocabulary was different, as was their manipulative gamesmanship. I was the one weak link out in the field that morning, and that was why I was so determined to handle the challenge myself.

I had ordered the shooters to remain posted in the four corners, two in front of and two behind the long line. A couple of them looked at me quizzically when I told them that the only shooting, if there was to be any, would be done by me. But Steve nodded in approval, understanding that I was not stripping them of their responsibility or authority, merely trying to assert mine. Nudging my horse slowly along the edge of the long line, I realized that I ran the risk of losing face if things did not go according to plan. The possibility that the prisoner might

Gun-toting convicts known as trusty shooters were a common sight at Parchman prior to federal intervention in the 1970s.

actually get past us had not entered my mind. By taking a rifle in my hands, however, I had assumed a personal role; if I did not handle it just right, I would never gain respect or credibility with either the inmates or the staff.

Standing up in the stirrups, I strained to see across the endless field of green, searching for the slightest movement that would give the inmate's presence away. The cotton was absolutely motionless, the heavy Delta air devoid of the slightest breeze. As I looked at my watch I reminded myself to remain patient. It had been nearly ten minutes and still no sign of movement. I knew that time was my ally, but I was nervous and anxious for it to be over with. Then, just as I turned my horse in the direction of the shooter a few yards away, the affair ended even more quickly than it had begun. Steve began shouting first, and instantly the other shooters joined in. I looked in the direction they excitedly pointed to, still unable to see the inmate. But he was apparently crawling rapidly, and the tops of some cotton plants halfway across the line were clearly moving. Raising my rifle and inhaling deeply, I slowly began to squeeze the trigger. I hesitated momentarily, wondering if firing a shot would spook my horse. (I could just see myself being dragged off by a runaway steed!) Not the time to worry, I thought. In a flash I fired, having taken dead aim at the chestnut-sized cotton bolls that just a moment before had been dancing in the sun. The inmate started hollering not to shoot, gradually rising from his hiding place, hands on top of his head. The two shooters closest to him sped across the field, reining in the horses ever so slightly. Yelling instructions, with weapons pointed just inches away, they escorted him toward me, their horses pushing him into a full trot across the clod-laden Delta soil. Laying the rifle across the saddle, I silently whispered a prayer of thanks. The horse had never flinched!

The usual practice with inmates who had tried to flee was to transfer them to "Little Alcatraz," the maximum security/death row unit. Prisoners did not like going there, and it usually required no more than a few days before they were ready to return to their camp and behave themselves. For those hard-shell cases who were either too dangerous or too unruly to live in other camps, the confines of the maximum security unit became their entire world. It was a dark existence based on fear, intimidation, and violence that victimized inmates and staff alike.

The would-be "rabbit" standing before me was a scrawny little kid, his sandy hair wet from sweat and his freckled face beet red from the heat, covered with dirt from head to toe. Inquiring how old he was, I was not in the least surprised when he said he would soon be seventeen. He was not sure what he was trying to do—run, he guessed; but he did not know where to run and claimed he just did it on impulse. He acknowledged that his foolishness could easily have gotten him killed. As I sat on my horse looking down at him, I thought how unfortunate it was to see such a youngster in prison. Further questioning revealed that he was from North Carolina and had stolen a car while hitchhiking through Mississippi. The local judge had given him three years, he said, to teach him not to steal cars. The boy—trembling visibly, shaken at having been shot at, apologizing—assured me that if I let him stay in camp I would have no more problems with him. His youthfulness made him a less than ideal candidate for the maximum security unit. But before I would agree to let him stay, I wanted the truth behind his escape attempt. The swollen, red, puffy area under one of his eyes had not escaped my attention. It had not been missed, either, by one of the shooters who brought him to me—he had whispered his considered opinion that the boy was having problems at night in the cage.

Ordering the long line back to work, I pulled the boy off to the side and asked him to tell me the real reason behind his attempted escape. He feigned total ignorance, saying he did not know why he ran. I knew it was unlikely he was going to tell me his reasons, especially since I was questioning him within view of a hundred other convicts. He did not want to wear a "snitch jacket," to become known among the inmates as an informant. Finally, I told him to get back in line and return to work, which he did quite agreeably. All things considered, the matter had gone well. The men in the line got the message that although I could be pretty easy to get along with, I also possessed the ability and determination to carry out the more unpleasant aspects of my job. My stock also rose considerably in the eyes of the shooters. They knew that I could be fair and understanding, but "mean as a junkyard dog" (as one so succinctly stated) when the situation required it.

That evening I detailed the incident to Tom Bennett. He praised my handling of the situation and directed me to submit a written report. As I left the camp later, having given the inmate my word that he would be allowed to avoid punishment in the maximum security unit, I naïvely believed the incident was behind me. But the next morning, as the inmates lined up to march off to the fields, I did not see him. I went back inside and told the cage boss to find him for me. The burly inmate flashed a toothless grin and told me the sergeant had transferred the boy the night before. My jaw tightened as I attempted to repress my anger. I had given my word to the inmate that he would not be transferred, and I had told that to Bennett the previous evening. There were frequent rumors about the maximum security unit, rumors of inmates being physically abused by both trusties and staff. But at the moment I was more concerned with my ability to make a promise to an inmate and keep it. True enough, I thought, Tom Bennett was the boss, but he had put me in charge of the long line. If I was to be held accountable for disciplining inmates in my work crew, then I should have some voice in how they were to be handled. I was ready to confront my supervisor that morning, but he had not yet come to camp when I moved the long line out. After the escape attempt the day before, the line seemed to step just a bit livelier than usual. Except for a whispered exchange now and then, the usual chatter and horseplay were largely absent.

We had been in the fields a couple of hours when Bennett's familiar red pickup approached, a cloud of dust trailing behind it. I made no attempt to meet him at the field's edge, wanting him to sense my anger. Finally, after he had walked about seventy-five yards down the rows, I steered my horse in his direction. As he walked up to me, hands in his hip pockets, he smiled and made some small talk about how good the cotton looked. Grunting my agreement, I leaned forward, resting my arms on the saddle horn. Bennett took out a bandanna and wiped the sweat from his forehead, chuckling all the while. He clearly knew I was angry, and he knew why. Leonard, Bennett's canteen man (and, in inmate slang, his "main most snitch"), had told him. I knew before leaving camp that morning that Leonard would report my displeasure to Tom as soon as he could. I intended that he do so.

I continued staring impassively while the sergeant explained why he had ordered the boy moved—to be punished the same as any other inmate who tried to escape. Suddenly, his smile was replaced by a scowl that revealed the seriousness with which he regarded my attitude. Kicking at a dirt clod, he put his hands on his hips and began to chew me out. I was paid to guard convicts, he said, not to make policy. The warden's policy was to punish inmates who attempted to escape. Bennett chided me for having displayed my anger in front of inmates that morning. Such behavior merely made our jobs more difficult, he fumed. Inmates would take advantage of any perceived weakness in the system, including dissension among prison staff. Tom never raised his voice, never uttered one expletive. But he quickly reminded me, in a way that certainly humbled me, who was boss. I turned the horse around and got back to my duties. I had just received a lesson in the prison school of hard knocks.

Although Tom Bennett did not have the formal education or administrative experience of Charlie Gaughan, he was no less impressive at letting me know who the boss was. Despite his laid-back appearance, he would not be pushed around by anyone, especially by a wise-cracking Yankee who thought he knew everything about prisons. Years later, when I returned to Parchman as warden, Tom and I would laugh heartily whenever we recounted the early days of our working relationship, weeks and months that had indeed been a rude awakening. But, with Tom Bennett's help, I became a better corrections employee because of them. Even though I would continue to find myself at philosophical odds with Tom on many occasions during my service under him, we managed to forge a genuine respect for each other and, more importantly, a true friendship.

Delta Blues

Well, my good fellow, you understand these things;
what ought I to do?

Socrates

By 1984 I had fulfilled my dream of occupying the warden's chair at Parchman. Time moved to a different beat there, yet the days were never quite long enough. Operating a prison that holds nearly six thousand men and employs half again as many staff leaves a warden little time for luxuriating. It had taken twelve years of hard work, determination, and planning, with a few detours along the way; but always, the goal had been the same. I never wavered in believing that my time would come.

When the chance did arrive, it also put me face to face with the hard realities of the death penalty. Even though it would still be many months before Edward Earl Johnson's execution, I found myself acutely aware of the prospect. Several times we had begun preparations, only to "stand down" late in the process because the inmate had won a new appeal. Eventually, however, on an early morning in 1987 the news would come that we were going to have an execution and that there would be no delays.

It began like any one of a thousand other days at Parchman. Up before dawn, I made rounds through several camps before the inmates went to breakfast at 5:30. These early morning hours were my favorite part of the day, affording me the chance to move casually among both inmates and guards. This was a time when I could relax and be myself before having to face the bureaucratic onslaught.

Later that morning, right after ending my daily meeting with the deputy wardens, a phone call came from Marvin "Sonny" White, an assistant attorney general. He was the state's lead counsel on death penalty cases. Sonny and I rarely worked with each other, though he had warned me several weeks earlier that Mississippi would likely have an execution "very soon."

Sonny was a pleasant guy, one of the few lawyers for whom I ever developed a real fondness. Unlike many attorneys, his personality was low-key, but he could be forceful and persuasive when necessary. One reason I liked him so much was that we had some traits in common. It pleased me no end that, like me, Sonny suffered from thinning hair and an expanding girth (although his six-foot frame seemed to handle it much more gracefully than my five feet seven inches). More important, he was self-assured enough to be able to poke fun at himself.

White's greeting was friendly enough, but somewhat restrained, and his lack of attorney-like bombast let him come directly to the point. I was really not shocked by his announcement that an execution was imminent. Edward Earl Johnson had been on the row for more than six years and had exhausted his appeals. Before hanging up, Sonny advised me that this execution would be just the first; there would be others before the year was over, perhaps as many as three or four. The state supreme court was to meet the next day, he said, at which time they would set a date.

Mindful of the controversy that had clouded Mississippi's last execution, four years earlier, every detail, however minor, was reviewed again and again. Tests were conducted on the gas chamber to make sure it was mechanically sound; procedures were practiced, revised, and practiced again. If it was at all preventable, there would be no debacles like the Jimmy Lee Gray execution on my watch.

In spite of telling myself many times that I was just "doing my job," as Johnson's date with death loomed closer I increasingly felt the crush of events. The planning and meticulous attention to detail paid off, however, and Edward Johnson's execution came off flawlessly. There was just one problem. Afterward, I felt dirty. I remember standing in the shower at three o'clock in the morning, scrubbing as hard as I could. No matter what I tried, nothing seemed to put my mind at ease. The rest of the world could afford to be matter-of-fact, I thought;

they had not strapped a man in a chair and killed him. I would remember every detail about Edward Earl Johnson—every wrinkle, every blemish—forever. I tried convincing myself that the process would become easier with each execution . . . that I would become "used" to it . . . hardened by it all.

Soon I heard from Sonny White again, alerting me that preparations should begin for another execution. Though not surprised by his call, I was stunned by the news of who was to be executed next. As I pensively lowered the telephone, the names and faces of nearly five dozen condemned prisoners flashed through my mind. How, I wondered, could a Marion Pruett continue to cheat the gas chamber, while the cold hand of fate reached out to others who were far less deserving? Pruett, tagged by the press as "Mad Dog," was a cold-blooded killer who was thought to have murdered at least a half dozen people for the sheer pleasure of it. The process of determining who took the last walk and who did not left me more than a little bewildered.

I summoned Deputy Wardens Steve Puckett and Dwight Presley to my office, and we quickly began planning for the next execution. "Jesus," Presley exclaimed, "we just had one. Is this going to become some kind of damned habit?" Steve Puckett, meanwhile, stood silently, looking out the office window. Hands resting on his hips, the tall, boyish-looking Puckett turned and asked, "Who is it this time?"

Flopping down into the high-backed swivel chair, accidentally banging the credenza behind me, I sighed loudly. Clenching a fist in anger, I pounded the massive oak desk that had been used by so many other wardens before me. I had wondered, long ago, what it would feel like to sit behind the impressive desk; now, I knew only too well.

Of all the inmates on the row, there was only one that I had allowed myself to become close to, to get to know as an individual. Strange as it may seem, I had come to regard him as a friend. Cursing softly, I asked aloud, of no one in particular, "Why, out of all the guys on the row, why does it have to be this one?" Steve Puckett immediately knew who I was talking about. "Damn," he muttered, "Connie's a good boy, damn it!" Dwight Presley turned and reached for the door. Bitterly, he proclaimed how unfair it was to "nail Connie when bastards like Pruett deserve it so much more."

Within an hour, I found myself shuffling down the cellblock, preparing to deliver the news to Connie Ray Evans. He was a quiet guy, always polite and respectful and really well liked by the other cons, as well as by the staff. If ever a death row had a soul, it could be found in Connie Evans, of that much I was convinced.

The correctional officer who walked beside me chattered idly, though I did not hear much of what he said. Lost in thought, I passed the cells of three inmates who were housed in the unit not as condemned prisoners but as security risks. Thinking about their case filled me with anger. While being held in a county jail near Jackson, they had concocted an escape plan, one that bore all the earmarks of tragedy. Because the young desperadoes had been transported back and forth to court numerous times by the local sheriff's department, they had gotten ample opportunity to look for weak points in the security procedures. Sadly, the entire transportation process was an invitation to disaster.

The sheriff's patrol vehicles did not all have rear screens behind which prisoners could be placed when being transported. These screens are considered essential in most agencies, but are out of financial reach for many rural departments that are strapped for funds.

The three inmates had also observed that they were usually handcuffed in front, rather than behind their bodies. As one of them told me later, they did not create the circumstances, they merely took advantage of them. After several months in the county jail, the three inmates were scheduled to be returned to the penitentiary. During their trip back to Parchman, they overpowered the lone deputy who was transporting them. Forcing the vehicle off the road, they were not content simply to escape—they coldly murdered the deputy with his own service revolver, discarding the man's body in a ditch, like garbage.

Their crime was not one of passion borne of jealousy or anger, nor was it the result of a robbery gone bad. Planned in advance and carried out ruthlessly, it was a crime that possessed all the trappings of an execution. Yet none of the three criminals received the death penalty—they had been fortunate enough to commit the heinous act in a county that had not rendered a death verdict in more than forty years. All had received life sentences and would be eligible for parole in ten years.

Connie Ray Evans was not quite as lucky. He committed his murder in a county where juries did not hesitate to impose the death penalty. He was also unfortunate enough to have had an accomplice who testified against him in return for an unusually lenient sentence. Approaching his cell to tell him of his date with the executioner, I wondered what set Evans apart from the three men I had just passed. What made him more deserving of death than them?

The cellblock was noticeably quiet, save for the sound of the officer rattling the ring of keys in his hand. How very different it had been when I patrolled the same cellblocks so many years before. I shook my head in disbelief as I remembered the less than sterling circumstances that led to my transfer and initial introduction to Parchman's death row late in the summer of 1972.

Life was never easy in Parchman's notorious camps back then, but after the lights went out at night they became arenas of debauchery and lawlessness. During the nighttime hours, the dormitories were ruled by cagebosses. They and their henchmen lorded it over the other inmates through threats, intimidation, and violence. Cagebosses were handpicked by the camp sergeants specifically for their ability and willingness to rule by fear. Inmates foolish enough to cross swords with a cageboss often became the victims of so-called accidental injuries. Like canteen operators, cagebosses were among the sergeant's most loyal inmate advisors. Even though civilian guards were employed in the camps at night, they seldom ventured inside the dormitories, or "cages," as they were commonly called. The guards largely relied on the cagebosses to maintain law and order.

I had taken a strong dislike to Tom Bennett's cagebosses as the result of several run-ins with them, the last one leading to my transfer from the camp. One night, tired of tossing and turning, I decided to go to the camp and make an unexpected trip through the dormitories. Having been assigned there for several months, I knew most of the inmates, especially the trusties. Those who were Sergeant Bennett's most trusted allies were polite and respectful, but they kept their distance from me. I knew that my middle-of-the-night visit would give the cageboss and some of the trusties information to report to Bennett later in the morning, but I was too disgusted with the situation to care.

As I entered the camp's front gate, the inmate shooter started to call inside to notify the night watchman. If he did, I warned sternly, he would find himself transferred to a gunman camp before morning, a fate trusties feared more than any other. (Gunmen, the inmates who were guarded by the shooters, did not feel kindly toward trusties.)

It was not really my intention to sneak into the camp unnoticed, but, knowing the old night watchman as I did, I wanted to surprise him with an unexpected wake-up call. I hung around the front gate a few minutes, casually chatting with Pappy, the bespectacled shackshooter whose fifty years or so of hard living clearly showed in his face. Suddenly a commotion of some kind erupted inside; although I could hear several voices shouting, I was not able to distinguish what was being said. Pappy chuckled, shaking his head as he mentioned matter-of-factly that the old man had been hollering at the cons all night. Well known by staff and inmates for his intemperate behavior and volatile outbursts, the night watchman had been assigned at one time or another to just about every camp in the penitentiary. He had even been known to fire his rifle into the cages on occasion, just because the inmates were "talking too loud."

In many ways Parchman was still foreign to me, despite my having worked there for several months. In Massachusetts the guards carried weapons and enforced rules, not the inmates; in the Alice-in-Wonderland world of the Mississippi State Penitentiary it was quite the reverse. The level of lawlessness within inmate dormitories defied belief. The unwritten rule was that employees did not venture into the cages after lights-out; defiantly, if not foolishly, I pretty much ignored it. Of course, Bennett had chided me, after discovering my first sojourn, for "undermining" the authority of the cageboss. My refusal to permit this trusty to accompany me as I made rounds late one night had incensed him, causing a prompt report of my actions to Bennett. After that, the cageboss and I waged a private war. Not content to let a sleeping dog lie, the next time I entered the cage, a few nights later, I woke the cageboss and told him that if he snitched on me to the sergeant again I would find a way to "jackpot" him right out of the camp.

The irascible night watchman was never really pleased to see me either, always hollering for me to get my "nosy ass out or get it whipped." Usually, it was pretty difficult to figure out who ran to Bennett the quickest following my intrusive visits, the watchman or the cageboss. The old man was far less circumspect than the inmate in his criticism, often telling Tom Bennett that I was nothing but a "shit-stirring damned Yankee."

I had come to take great delight in knowing that my mere presence enraged him so. Somewhat naïvely, I supposed that if I were ever injured or killed while working at Parchman it would be at the hands of a resentful cageboss or even a night watchman.

Bidding Pappy a mischievous farewell, I slipped into the camp unnoticed and stood in the entranceway. The night watchman was standing at the cage bars, engaged in a typically boisterous conversation, arms flailing in all directions. I spied the young inmate who was arguing back so vociferously, and immediately recognized him. He was the same youngster, the North Carolina car thief, who had made a halfhearted escape attempt in the fields just weeks earlier. Neither he nor the night watchman had yet detected my presence. Eager not to interrupt the inopportune scene, I quietly tapped on the door to the canteen, which was just to my left. Leonard, the tall, powerfully built canteen operator, opened the door, his eyes registering surprise at my presence. Signaling him with a finger over my lips to remain quiet, I quickly entered the darkened room, nearly stumbling over his bunk as I made my way to the canteen window. Having been awakened by the commotion, Leonard had raised the service window, enabling him (and me) to observe everything.

The two continued to shout at each other, their sharp exchanges awakening other inmates. Across the dining room, several trusties were standing at the bars, placidly watching the commotion. I was lighting a cigarette when the boyish inmate unexpectedly began wailing. Leonard whispered that the brouhaha had been going on for at least half an hour. "What the hell is it all about?" I whispered. He sighed, responding with an uncharacteristic hint of concern in his voice. "The cageboss and some of his buddies have been threatening all night to fuck him." Puffing on my cigarette, I peered across the dayroom, watching the old man strike viciously at the inmate's hands, tightly wrapped around the bars, with the butt of his rifle. The boy

hung on, screaming for the night watchman not to let the other inmates get him. A shudder went down my spine as I listened to him
plead with the watchman not to let them take him off to the showers.
"Please, please mister, don't let them fuck me!" the boy cried out hysterically. "Don't let them do it!" The old man threw back his head and
laughed hideously, again hitting the boy's hands with the rifle butt
with all the force he could muster. Cursing and laughing at the same
time, the watchman contemptuously told the inmate, "Don't worry,
boy, you're so damned ugly there ain't no convict in there that'd want
to fuck you."

I had seen and heard enough. As I turned to leave the canteen, the
boy shrieked again, crying hysterically as the cageboss and three of his
buddies pummeled and kicked him into partial submission. Leonard
urged me to hurry. I looked at him with surprise and suspicion, for we
did not especially like each other. I knew he had snitched on me to
Tom Bennett more than once, providing me with ample reason to distrust him. As if reading my thoughts, Leonard mumbled apologetically,
"No matter what you think of me, it ain't right to stand by and let a
young kid get gang-banged by a bunch of thugs."

I purposely slammed the canteen door behind me, hollering at the
night watchman, who was leaning back in his rickety swivel chair.
Somewhat startled but obviously unimpressed, the old man never
flinched, even though his laid-back posture conveyed a little too much
calmness. I wondered what there was about the man that made me dislike him so intensely. Of course, the feeling was mutual, probably de-
servedly, for I did very little to hide my disdain. He was always dishev-
eled, his white shirt a yellowing patchwork of coffee and tobacco
stains. Squinting behind his black-framed glasses, his rheumy eyes
were usually bloodshot. The gray stubble on his ruddy, craggy face was
streaked with tobacco juice that had collected in the corners of his
mouth. He reached for his makeshift spittoon, a discarded soda can, as
I casually asked what was going on. At first he merely grunted, rocking
the squeaky chair back and forth. Suddenly bolting upright, he hissed
through gritted teeth that "whatever the bastard gets, he deserves."

Other inmates began to stir from their beds, a few coming up to
the cage bars and shouting obscenities. By no stretch of the imagina-

tion were their protests to be confused with concern for a fellow convict. They could not have cared less about the beating that was being administered by the cageboss and his friends. In the big house men quickly learn to mind their own business. Two cardinal rules of the convict code were not to snitch and not to stick your nose into another inmate's business. No, they were merely upset that their sleep was being interrupted by all the racket.

Spinning around, I testily told the inmates at the bars to shut up and return to their bunks. I then shouted for the cageboss and his cohorts to let the boy go. Ignoring me, the shadowy figures continued to pummel their victim, dragging him to the rear of the dormitory as they did so. No one attempted to intervene. Though fearful that the same thing could happen to them, the other cons were even more afraid of what might happen should they interfere in another inmate's trouble.

I told the night watchman to throw me the keys. Having realized by now that I had apparently witnessed the entire incident, however, he started rambling again. In his loud, raspy voice (and spraying tobacco juice everywhere), he asserted that the inmate was a troublemaker who "needs to get his ass whipped." Angrily, I reached to snatch the keys off the table, but Leonard, who had followed me out of the canteen, had already retrieved them and he quickly tossed them to me. The old man launched into another venomous rant, threatening to kill me if I interfered. Concerned about the rifle in his hands and the smell of alcohol on his breath, I was hardly eager to get into a wrestling match with him. Under the best of circumstances, the night watchman's behavior was often unpredictable, if not downright bizarre. I could not be sure that he would not use the gun to reinforce his threat; he just might be crazy enough, I thought, to do it.

But then the old man gave me a big break. Infuriated by my interference, he threw the rifle down on the table and stormed out of the camp. Leonard, who had retreated back to the canteen, reappeared in the dining hall with a riot baton in his hand. Apprehensively, I threw the keys back to him, shouting instructions to let my long-line shooters out of the trusty cage. I stepped back to the cage and flipped the wall switch, turning all the dormitory lights on. Picking up the rifle, I shoved it at Steve, my lead shooter. Anxiously, I told him to give me five minutes to get the boy out of the cage before calling the security dispatcher for assistance. Leonard asked if he should call Sergeant Bennett, while Steve warned me against entering the cage alone. "No!" I snapped in response to Leonard. I knew the sergeant would have to be called, but there was no time right then.

The cage door opened quickly, and I turned to throw the keys back to one of the shooters. I was holding the riot baton so tightly that my fingers were turning white. It was decidedly quiet in the cage, save for an occasional murmur that drifted from a bed here or there. The air hung motionless, heavy with the odor of stale sweat and dirt. Row upon row of crowded bunks, separated only by homemade partitions of cardboard boxes, afforded little privacy. Every so often, a curious face would peer from behind one of the mildewed towels that hung alongside the beds. Some inmates were sitting upright, silently watching, waiting patiently to see who would win the confrontation, although the outcome would be of little consequence to most of them.

I did not know for sure what I was going to do. One prison guard with a riot baton is not much of a match for four or five hostile inmates. While I could not be positive, I had to presume that at least some of the inmates might be armed with "shanks," or homemade prison knives. I also had to worry that other inmates might suddenly decide to join in, lending assistance to the cageboss and his cohorts.

When I was halfway down the aisle, an inmate suddenly came out of the shower area. Startled for a moment, I soon recovered and ordered him to step out into the aisle; instead, he quickly turned and disappeared back into the shower area. I continued cautiously, turning toward the showers, which were just a few yards away. Without warning, the cageboss and his three cohorts stepped from behind a wall that separated the showers from the latrine area. One of the trio, Malcolm, was a short, grubby-looking man who walked with a limp—a chronic troublemaker with an obnoxiously loud mouth. He and the two other inmates standing to the immediate right of the cageboss stepped out in front. Belligerently, Malcolm then took another step toward me; I ordered him to walk over to the wall and place his hands above his head. The convict stared at me intently, eyes filled with anger and contempt, and stood motionless.

So what now, I thought. Common sense suggested that I might want to just turn around and slowly walk out; this presumed, of course, that the cons would permit me such a luxury. And I knew that, much as I might want to, I could not do that. For lack of any better ideas, I ordered them, in a very bellicose manner, to "catch the wall." The cageboss immediately became a spokesperson, trying to explain that they had not hurt the inmate, just given him a little "spanking" (convict slang for roughing the boy up).

Fortunately, the other inmates had not injected themselves into the battle of nerves yet, though I could feel a hundred pairs of eyes staring at me. Cutting the cageboss off in midsentence, I threatened to take his head off with the riot baton if he and the other three did not immediately do exactly as they were told. Even while yelling instructions, I knew only too well that I had placed myself at a severe disadvantage. Much to my amazement and relief, however, three of them, including the cageboss, all but ran to the wall; but Malcolm could not back down—not in front of all those other cons. It did not take me long to realize that words were not going to work with him. Without warning, I took a couple of steps forward and struck him with all the force I could muster, bringing the riot baton down squarely across his shinbone. I bellowed at the others not to move lest they receive the same. Stepping over Malcolm, who had crumpled to the concrete floor in pain, I found the young inmate in the shower. He was scared as hell, rolled up in a ball in the corner, trembling uncontrollably. There had not really been much time to beat him before they were interrupted, although his face and head had been worked over thoroughly with a "lock in a sock." A favorite tactic of convicts when administering a beating to another prisoner, this involves no more than tying a padlock, or even a bar of soap, inside a sock and swinging it as a weapon. It was a very effective and painful technique, especially when applied around the head and shoulders.

Helping the boy to his feet, I escorted him from the shower to the dormitory. Then, with his four assailants in front of us, we all walked slowly down the central aisle and into the dining room. Realizing that I had not even taken time to pat-search the four inmates, I was more than a little anxious. Although they could have easily been carrying weapons, my first thought was simply to get them, the victim, and myself out of the cage without further incident. As it turned out, I was extremely fortunate that none of them was armed.

Once in the dayroom, I forcefully threw the cageboss and his friends facedown on the floor. After directing Steve to shoot the first one that moved, a rush of relief embraced me as I collapsed into the chair the night watchman had occupied just moments earlier. Mopping away beads of perspiration, I was surprised when I looked at my watch. Although it had felt like an eternity, the whole thing had taken less than three minutes.

At last I ambled over to the telephone and called central security, informing them that I had four inmates awaiting transfer to the Maximum Security Unit (MSU). Moments later the cageboss and his friends were whisked away, while the cause of their downfall was transported to the prison hospital to have his injuries attended to. It was almost two o'clock before the watch commander sent another officer to fill in for the departed night watchman, and by then I had decided that Tom Bennett could wait until morning.

Six o'clock came and went, minus my appearance to take the long line out, for I was still sound asleep. By six-thirty, however, one of the trusties was banging on my front door. Bennett had sent him to get me up with the expectation that I would be at work "momentarily." Johnny Hazlewood, the young man standing in my living room, scratched his head and, smiling shyly, told me that the sergeant was in a real bad mood. The word around the camp was that I would be on the road before the day was over.

I took my time showering and dressing. No need to get in a hurry now, I thought, the inmate rumor mill was probably correct, and I was probably about to be fired for not having called Bennett. Characteristically stubborn, I was even more convinced that morning that I had done the right thing. Had I waited for the sergeant to arrive, the young inmate could have been seriously injured or killed. Only two years earlier, a Parchman convict had died at the hands of other inmates. The administration initially attributed the death to heatstroke; two autopsies later, prison officials acknowledged that the boy had been beaten to death. While inmate murders are not uncommon, the killing of

Danny Bennett in 1970 was largely the result of the same kind of law-lessness that permeated Parchman in 1972, a prison culture that could have resulted in a similar tragedy the previous night.

A short time later I strode into the camp yard to find the inmates already lined up for their trek to the fields, their ranks abuzz with conversation about the previous night's activities. Entering the building, I was on edge from lack of sleep and restless anticipation of Tom Bennett's wrath. The sergeant was not in his office, but Leonard silently pointed me in the direction of the trusty cage. Shuffling across the dining hall, Tom made his way toward the front of the dayroom. Appearing somewhat contentious at first, Tom flashed his familiar grin and slapped me gently on the back. Everything was okay, or so I thought.

Explaining the previous night's trouble as I walked with him toward his office, we stopped in front of the camp's open doorway. The early morning sunlight streamed in, accompanied by a refreshing wave of cool air. Tom casually shook his head, reassuring me that he knew all about it and had since right after it happened. I looked at him quizzically, asking if the watch commander had notified him. Striking a familiar pose, he slid both hands into his back pockets and chuckled softly. The old night watchman, after storming out of the camp, had gone straight to Bennett's house. Apologetically, I offered to tell him why I had not called immediately, but Bennett shocked me by replying that he did not bother coming to the camp because he figured I was capable of handling things on my own.

Feeling quite pleased with myself, I thanked him and exuberantly walked outside to escort the long line to the fields. Reaching for the saddle horn to boost myself atop the waiting horse, I felt Tom Bennett's firm grasp on my shoulder. Almost in a whisper, his steely eyes piercing mine, he told me how very lucky I was. Had I ever heard of asking for help? His anger was unmistakable as he grabbed my arm and directed me back inside. I stood in his office sullen and silent, knowing that it was not a time for me to talk. His anger boiled over. The penitentiary was no place for showing off, he gruffly asserted. I had no right to jeopardize myself the way I had; even if I did, what of my responsibility to my family? Mincing no words and sparing no feelings, Bennett hit hardest where he knew it would hurt most. I had a wife and a fifteen-month-old son, with another baby on the way. One man with a riot baton does not go after four convicts, convicts who may be armed, and usually are! Clearly agitated, Tom jabbed his finger in my chest for added emphasis. It was not enough that I decided to take on four convicts by myself. I had to do it inside a dormitory full of a hundred others!

Trying to think of something to say that would make sense, I attempted again to apologize, but the sergeant would have none of it. I owed him nothing, he exclaimed. If there was a need to apologize for my foolish actions the night before, perhaps, he suggested sarcastically, I should offer apologies to my family for having taken such an unwise and unnecessary risk.

He was right, and deep down I knew he was right. I should have called him; what's more, I should have called for backup. But everything happened so fast, I told myself, there was no time to think. That was the gist of Tom's concern—I did not think. Penitentiaries are fraught with danger for those who showboat. Bennett was in no mood to listen to explanations, and I was too embarrassed to pursue the issue right then. I thought it best to take the long line out to the fields and stay out of my supervisor's hair for a while.

About midmorning, Tom drove out to the fields to tell me that my presence was requested in John Collier's office. My first thought was that I was about to be fired, but then I remembered that the warden did not often bother to meet with guards before firing them. They were usually just told by the camp sergeant to clear out and hit the road. Tom Bennett feigned ignorance of the reasons for my being called up front. Most assuredly, he was more than a little upset about his cageboss being locked down. I was certain he had complained either to Associate Warden Jack Byars or Chief of Security Danny K. Thomas, for, I bitterly concluded, it was obvious that he would rather lose me than some damned convict thug.

A short time later I entered Collier's office, and waited nervously for Laura Newsome, his secretary, to finish whispering the latest bit of prison gossip to another employee from the nearby records office. Laura, a plain and not particularly friendly woman, briefly interrupted her animated conversation and tersely instructed me to wait in the lobby. About twenty anxious minutes passed before I was finally ushered into Collier's office. I had been there only once before, but it was evident that he had done some impressive remodeling. The windows were set off by rather lavish drapes, and as he leaned back I could not help noticing his luxurious leather chair. The desk, however, had not changed. It was still the biggest I had ever seen, taking up most of the room. For a second, I wondered what it would be like to sit on the other side, but at that moment I was convinced I would never find out.

The warden wasted no time with pleasantries. I was being moved to the death row unit immediately. Certain people (whom he declined to name) cared neither for my correctional philosophy nor for some of my methods. I sat perfectly motionless, my heart pounding in my ears, as John Collier's words struck like a cannonade. Try as I might to reconcile myself to what was happening, I steadfastly refused to acknowledge that I deserved to be punished. Staring blankly past the man on the other side of the vast oak desk, I felt weighted down by the full force of his bureaucratic trappings and authority. Collier, normally so even tempered, was uncharacteristically irate. Obviously I had managed to incur his full wrath. After listening to his tirade for a good ten minutes, I finally managed to attempt a mild protest, but he cut me off unceremoniously. Bristling at my ill-timed interruption, he bellowed at me to accept my reassignment to the death row unit and keep my mouth shut. Almost as an afterthought, he let me know that Tom Bennett had not requested my transfer. If Collier's intent had been to humble me, he had succeeded.

My spirit bruised and bleeding, I left the warden's office with his stinging admonition ringing in my ears. In spite of never directly referring to the previous night's incident, his message was crystal clear. I had not even the slightest doubt that I was fortunate to still have a job. Driving back to the First Offender's Unit for the final time, I did some serious soul-searching. How else could I have handled the situation? What was I to have done, stand idly by and permit four thugs to beat up or rape some kid barely old enough to have peach fuzz on his chin? Oh, hell, I knew that Bennett was right about one thing; I should never have entered the cage alone—not to take on four inmates. The cardinal rule for any correctional officer was always to wait for backup before wading into a confrontation with inmates. I stubbornly insisted that doing things by the book did not always work, but my argument had been dismissed. It was one of the hardest lessons I had to learn in corrections. Ironically, years later as a warden, I too would frown on officers who chose to risk their lives by acting alone.

The next morning seemed to arrive earlier than usual. Entering the death row unit for the first time, I found "Little Alcatraz" frightening enough. But what really caught my attention was the odor. All prisons have an almost aseptic smell—smells from years' worth of janitorial chemicals applied to floors, walls, and windows, combined with the musty odor of crowded, perspiring bodies. But the smell in Parchman's death row unit was unlike any I had ever experienced, except for the stench of Viet Nam.

Most of the officers were pretty friendly, and the sergeant was a good person to work for. Pat Mooney was a veteran of many years in corrections, both at Parchman and in California. One officer who particularly befriended me was Charlie Cole. About my age, he was of immense value in helping me learn the various nuances that were peculiar to the unit. In reality, my adjustment to death row went pretty smoothly. It was, after all, very familiar stuff—the cellblocks, the types of inmates that were housed there—much like the prisons I had cut my teeth on in Massachusetts.

Technically speaking, there was no death row anymore, since the Supreme Court had, earlier that summer, outlawed capital punishment. Although inmates who were on the row at the time of the Court's decision had their sentences commuted to life, many were still housed there. Wisely, the administration was evaluating the inmates individually to determine what other camps, if any, they could safely be transferred to.

As Charlie Cole correctly pointed out that first day, the prisoners who had been under sentence of death seldom posed any serious behavior problems. The real troublemakers were inmates who were housed on the former death row because of their recalcitrant behavior in other camps or their designation as severe security risks.

Most prisons have their share of bad days, but in the death row unit I sometimes wondered if I was working in a maximum security cellblock or an asylum. Though working conditions were poor in all the camps, death row was in many ways, the bottom of Parchman's barrel. In particular, the row often seemed beyond control, a situation that stemmed in large part from the general environment of the place. Trusties performed many of the chores on the cellblocks, such as handing out meals, mail, and medications. They were also responsible for handing out a lot of discipline in the form of corporal punishment. Unquestionably, the trusties went out of their way to antagonize their fellow prisoners.

After a couple of weeks, I gave up trying to figure out if the inmates arrived on the row behaving like animals or if the unit made them that way. Just working in the place was degrading. The environment was charged with anger and open hatred between convicts and guards. Inmates routinely threw feces and urine at us, flooded their cells, and stopped up toilets. Officers and trusty workers—patience depleted and nerves frayed—responded with brute force. There was precious little that could be done under the existing circumstances. Guards simply tried to put in their hours, thankful, at the end of each day, for their survival.

Like the rest of Parchman, the death row unit had been neglected and ignored. But if legislators were reluctant to spend money on Parchman in general, the death row unit was at the bottom of everybody's priority list. Why spend money on cold-blooded murderers and recalcitrant inmates who refused to behave themselves in other camps? Of course, such a simplistic attitude failed to recognize that prison employees had to endure the same harsh conditions as the inmates. When we walked down the cellblocks, it was frequently necessary to wear raincoats and rubber boots; these afforded some protection against the torrent of urine and feces that repeatedly rained down on us.

Such inmate behavior did a lot to reshape my views and opinions, not to mention my actions. One convict in particular proved to be a constant management problem. He was very unpopular with the guards because he was doing time for killing a state trooper. Short, greasy haired, and seedy looking, he spent much of his time bragging about the murder and how he tortured his victim before "mercifully" killing him. It was his sole claim to fame, the only way for an otherwise obscure little man to feel like he had succeeded at something, anything! When not busy bragging, he was always creating problems. A ringleader among the rowdy cons in the unit, he was always among the first to throw feces or urine at us. As the days passed, I developed an intense dislike for him. A longtime drug addict, he perceived himself as a highly skilled manipulator, an expert at outwitting staff. His behavior was extremely predictable, however. His favorite tricks were to feign an illness or to injure himself. He would then be transported to the prison hospital, where, if he was lucky, he would receive some kind of painkiller. When he really craved a fix and could not get it any other way, he would cut his Achilles tendon. Like clockwork, he would be taken to the prison hospital, where the doctors would administer a painkiller while sewing up the back of his ankle.

After this had happened several times, the prison doctor decided to make it a less attractive option. Next time, the doctor came to death row. Normally, prison policy prohibited anyone except officers and trusties from entering the cellblocks, and Doctor Julio would not violate it to the extent of going into the cell to sew up the inmate's foot. Instead, with the help of an enormous trusty nicknamed Hercules, the inmate was restrained face down on his bunk while his legs were pulled through the cell bars. Doctor Julio immediately stitched up the fellow's ankle—without the benefit of anything except a needle and thread. Although the convict's rage and anger in the succeeding days was intense, and he splashed feces and urine with unusual ferocity, he never cut his tendons again.

The maximum security section of the death row unit was a different world from the rest of Parchman. The inmates who had been sent to it for disciplinary reasons were the very worst the system had to offer. Like the other officers assigned there, I just wanted to get through work relatively unscathed, taking things one day at a time. I vowed, however, that I was not going to work in the MSU forever, and that if Warden Collier ever offered me the opportunity to transfer back to a work camp I would seize it in a second!

As had become my pattern at Parchman, I did not work very long (less than three months) in the death row unit, but in that time I had actually managed to stay out of trouble with both the unit sergeant and the front office. One afternoon, quite unexpectedly, I was told to report to the administration building. Strolling into the administrative sanctuary that was John Collier's office, I saw my friend Tom Graf, the prison psychologist, sitting in the corner. The warden was on his feet, greeting me with a warm and vigorous handshake. Tom slid his chair closer, smiling and patting me on the back. Before I was even seated, Collier told me I was to be promoted on the first of the month. I was to become a correctional counselor, working with inmates as a case manager.

At first, I said nothing. Collier jokingly said he understood that I would be chagrined at the prospect of leaving the death row unit, but that I ought to be used to moving around. He was right—I was thrilled at the prospect of leaving the row! At the same time, though, I felt an overwhelming urge to shout, "I'm being promoted to *what?*" The job that the warden was talking about was the very one that had been promised to me in the first place. Oh, well, better late than not at all! All three of us enjoyed the moment, but none more than I. Still, Collier's sudden acknowledgment that I had actually been doing good work, at least good enough to justify a promotion, had me slightly puzzled. I suspected it was Tom Graf who got me out of the warden's doghouse, and it was Graf for whom I would be working. Without warning, my career at Parchman had taken another unforeseen twist.

My last day of work as a correctional officer in the death row unit was relaxed and uneventful. The sergeant had dispatched Charlie Cole and me to do some routine maintenance on the gas chamber.

In playful curiosity, Charlie and I turned valves, dropped levers, and even sat in the chair. He closed the chamber door while I struck a pose sitting in the steel chair known as the "black death." Closing my eyes tightly, I tried to imagine the terror that must grip a man—but how can anyone really know what it feels like, I thought. I wondered aloud how many had been strapped in the chair. The freckle-faced, sandy-haired Cole shook his head, replying in his distinctive drawl,

"Thirty something, I think." Eight years had passed since Parchman's gas chamber was last used in 1964.

Even as we took turns sitting in the chair, I could feel the humor quickly fading, becoming a terrible sense of dread. It was, after all, a frightful object whose sole purpose was to kill.

Leaving the chamber, I casually remarked to Charlie how glad I was that I would never have to execute anyone. The death penalty, after all, was dead. The Supreme Court had made it so.

A Season
of Change

We cannot anticipate a perfectly just society,
but we can continue to make the effort.

Michael E. Endres, Xavier University

The summer of 1972 had been a long and painful one for Parchman officials, who endured assaults on all fronts. The lawsuit of Nazareth Gates (alleging unconstitutional conditions at the institution) had generated much unwanted publicity, exposing the penitentiary's sordid history of brutality, political interference, and administrative indifference. Ultimately, the case never went to trial (the state agreed to a settlement in December 1972), but a summer full of endless contempt hearings left prison officials in court and Parchman on the front pages of Mississippi's daily newspapers.

If negative publicity stemming from the federal court hearings was not sufficient fodder for critics of the prison, a series of calamities forced Parchman administrators even more on the defensive. John Allen Collier, as warden, bore the brunt of legislative and media outrage over the problems at the sprawling complex. Two high-profile escapes that summer underscored the extent of his difficulties. One involved a convicted murderer who had vowed to return to his hometown to kill his sentencing judge. For almost a week, prison and law enforcement authorities conducted one of the most intensive manhunts ever witnessed in Mississippi; state troopers moved into the judge's home to protect him and his family. The inmate was finally recaptured without incident—within earshot of the penitentiary. He had never even come close to the judge's residence, which was located several hundred miles from Parchman. The damage had been done, however, and the public relations nightmare simply grew worse for an embattled Collier administration.

Soon after that, another escape occurred that further wounded the warden's faltering credibility. Again, a convicted murderer was on the loose. This fellow was a trusty who had been granted some rather extraordinary privileges. He had, for instance, been permitted to keep his personal automobile at the penitentiary. So that it might be properly watched over, the vehicle was parked (when not being used by its inmate owner) behind the warden's residence. Unsettling as such an arrangement may have been to some in the administration, it made perfect sense to Collier. The convict was an experienced crop duster, a skill the warden thought to be of quite some value to the institution. Thousands of acres of Parchman's fertile farmland, planted in cotton and vegetables, required considerable aerial spraying. The trusty, Blue, was just the sort of man who was needed. Experienced farmer that he was, Collier knew a good thing when he saw it, or so he thought. The only problem was that Parchman did not have an aircraft of its own (the penitentiary had always let out contracts to private pilots for aerial spraying). John Collier had the ideal solution—he would let the prison use his own aircraft, with which he sprayed his farm. By making use of Blue's talents to perform the prison crop-dusting chores, the state would realize considerable savings. For a while the plan seemed to work flawlessly, and it became common to see the trusty flying the warden's crop duster over Parchman's far-flung fields. Blue took to his newly assigned task with a determination and vigor seldom seen among free men, let alone a convict serving life. He was in the air at the crack of dawn, and was often back performing his aerobatic feats again in the late evening.

No one, least of all the warden, thought much about Blue's wanderings; he was treated more like a valued employee than a convict. On more than a few occasions, the aircraft was prone to mechanical difficulties. Consequently, it was sometimes necessary to procure parts for it in Cleveland, Mississippi, about twenty miles from Parchman. Now, Blue was considered to be highly trustworthy by Collier—he was allowed to drive himself to town, in his own private vehicle, without escort, to conduct such business as was necessary to keep the airplane flying. Besides, the prison did not have anyone on the staff who could be spared just to drive a convict to Cleveland and back. The warden did not think he had any reason to doubt his most valued trusty. The inmate was allowed to go just about anywhere on the farm he wanted, whether in his own car or in the crop duster. He often worked on the airplane until very late at night, and he spent very little time in his assigned camp.

Unfortunately for John Collier, he forgot that his pilot-mechanic was a convict. To make matters worse, Blue had a drinking problem. He was not a bad convict, as convicts go, but he was a convict nonetheless. Eventually, the temptation became too great, and the inmate drove out Parchman's back gate one Friday morning toward freer pastures. That an inmate had escaped from the Mississippi State Penitentiary by driving his own vehicle as the guard merrily waved him through the gate was quite sufficient ammunition for John Allen Collier's critics. But insult was heaped upon injury when prison officials acknowledged that, even though Blue had left on a Friday, his escape had not been detected until the following Monday, when it occurred to one of the deputy wardens that he had not seen the inmate in several days. Upon being questioned, the guard on duty at the rear gate, where the escapee had left the prison, sheepishly acknowledged that though he clearly recalled Blue's departure he had no recollection of him ever returning. But neither did the guard have reason for suspicion. After all, the trusty had said he was going after some parts for the plane, and he had always come back before!

The incident emboldened critics in the Mississippi legislature, not to mention the media. Some legislators began to call openly for Governor Bill Waller to replace Collier, questioning both his qualifications and competence to serve as warden. The governor, however, continued to offer unflagging public support for John Collier.

Although the warden was experiencing considerable political difficulties, life for me had actually become tolerable as the summer wore on. All things considered, my transfer to the death row unit had turned out to be positive. The terrible working conditions there actually helped foster a spirit of cooperation among the officers that was rare elsewhere in the institution. Only after I had been away from Tom Bennett for a while, though, did I appreciate the full value of his practical knowledge and common sense. In retrospect, I was grateful for his patience and his tolerant sense of humor, despite his personal discomfort with some of my then liberal views of prisons and prisoners. Even though I remained convinced that he had campaigned to have me transferred out of his camp, I was thankful for the opportunity he had given me. The fact that it did not work out was not Tom's fault.

Quite the contrary, it was Bennett's willingness to allow me to learn by making mistakes that eventually served me well as I made the transition to working on the row. Officers there were often on their own, frequently called upon to make immediate decisions—decisions that could spell the difference between resolving a situation peacefully or bringing on chaos. Tom Bennett had not only permitted me to make decisions but, more importantly, he expected me to! More than most supervisors, he recognized the value of learning by doing, which inevitably included profiting from mistakes. Undeniably, Tom was often bewildered, if not outright displeased, with some of my decisions. I would have been chastised more severely, however, for failing to make any decisions at all. Sergeant Tom Bennett's philosophy fostered in me a willingness to exercise judgment and to act independently. Life on death row required officers to demonstrate a certain resolve, a willingness to act without waiting to be told. Inmates who were confined there on segregation status or who were in solitary confinement severely tested the patience and strength of purpose of the staff. Those guards who showed signs of weakness in their dealings with inmates did not survive the rigors of the row for long. Thankfully, Tom Bennett had prepared me well.

If ever I was presented with an opportunity to shed my label as a troublemaker, working on death row was it. Pat Mooney, the sergeant in charge of the unit, received the news of my arrival with a surprisingly positive attitude, a kind of "live and let live" philosophy. I was glad to still have a job, and he was equally grateful for another warm body to work in the unit.

The old adage that first impressions can be deceiving was never more true than in the case of Pat Mooney. Physically, he did not strike me as a man who supervised the most difficult unit in the penitentiary. About average in height, he could not have weighed more than 150 pounds. His face was almost gaunt looking, and he coughed constantly from his chain-smoking. A soft-spoken man who seldom found it necessary to raise his voice, Pat Mooney was a good person who was liked by almost everyone who knew him. So low-key were his demeanor and personality that it was difficult to imagine him married to his wife, who was strikingly different in both her personality and physical appearance. While Pat was a quiet, gangling fellow, his wife was brusque and forceful.

From my first day on the row I tried to heed John Collier's advice, maintaining a positive attitude and a very low profile. Although my assignment lasted slightly less than three months, it was, at least from the administration's point of view, considerably more successful than my previous engagement at the First Offender's Camp.

My continuing close friendship with Tom Graf ensured that I would never completely win the trust or confidence of many within Collier's administration. Tom's first great sin was that he was educated—worse yet, a psychologist. In most prisons, there has historically existed a wall of distrust between guards and so-called treatment staff. Such employees as case managers, counselors, chaplains, and teachers are often viewed as the enemy by the security staff. In the Parchman of 1972 there was more than a wall of distrust—there was contempt and outright hatred. Tom was a bright young professional, full of idealism and enthusiasm. He also had an infectious laugh and an indomitable sense of humor. But his keen intellect could also convey a biting sarcasm, often directed aggressively at an entrenched bureaucracy that he regarded with great disdain. Like me, he was considered an outsider, but perhaps even more so. At least I had the excuse of being from Massachusetts, a meddling Yankee who did not have enough sense to leave Parchman's affairs alone. Graf, on the other hand, was a native Mississippian, who could have reasonably been expected to understand and adhere to the social and bureaucratic codes that governed the penitentiary.

Although John Collier may have lacked management skills and formal training as a penologist, he was at times a most pragmatic individual. In his own peculiar way, he was also a visionary of sorts. Plainly, in the summer of 1972, significant change was in the offing. Despite strong personal objection to many of the rulings made by federal judge William Keady in nearby Greenville, the warden wisely declined to stand in the way of a legal juggernaut. Though not necessarily capable of always recognizing his most serious shortcomings, John Allen Collier unquestionably wanted to put his stamp on Parchman, perhaps to be remembered as the warden who bridged the gap between the old penology and the new. Yet in attempting to do so he faced an almost insurmountable difficulty. He was a farmer who had been appointed to the prison post without any prior experience in corrections.

In fairness to Collier, knowledge of prison administration had never been a real concern of Mississippi governors when selecting Parchman's wardens. After all, the mission of the penitentiary had always been primarily economic: to be frugal with state funds; to be self-supporting by raising and processing vegetables, beef, poultry, and pork; and to make a profit growing cotton. Good security, public safety, and humane treatment of prisoners were all subordinated to economic efficiency—the penitentiary was just one more large plantation.

Collier was shrewd enough, however, to recognize the growing need to have a professional penologist in his administration. As the prison psychologist, Tom Graf came closest to fulfilling this requirement. While it was difficult at times for the warden to embrace much of Graf's philosophy openly, he still welcomed him into his inner circle. Graf was a John Collier loyalist, though by no means a yes-man. Tom viewed his friendship with the warden as an allegiance, a responsibility to serve Collier with honesty, even if it meant an occasional disagreement. And the warden found himself in dire need of such integrity and candor, for he had discovered that he was surrounded by those who would, if possible, bring down his administration.

As for me, my brief stint on death row had been enough to convince Collier that he had been right in his decision to give me a second chance. Thanks in large part to Tom Graf's influence, I was assured of the warden's continuing support. My promotion to case manager, working directly under Graf, gained me even greater respect from and credibility with Collier. Being a case manager is, in most prisons, a pretty ordinary job, albeit an important one; such staffers are not usually included in the administrative braintrust. Yet, as in so many other ways, Parchman was different. I was the first case manager hired there, which had some distinct advantages. Most of the administration was not even sure what I was supposed to do. The warden leaned heavily on Graf in determining what my job was to encompass. (As it turned out, my duties were quite varied and rather broad.) I was exposed to every camp in the institution and to virtually every facet of the prison's operation. The position also afforded me an opportunity to learn a great deal more about inmates than I would have been able to as a correctional officer. Finally, as a case manager I had access to information in official records, material that was very often filled with revealing details of criminal life outside the walls and with the aberrations of prison life hidden deep within Parchman's camps.

The most significant thing that John Collier did for me, however, came in the form of an innocuous-appearing appointment to the penitentiary classification committee. Though not overly impressed at first with the added duty, I soon realized that the new job had its benefits. My presence on the prison staff suddenly became much more tolerable to some of the people who had worked so diligently to get rid of me. Not that I had become popular—if anything, their distrust had grown more intense. An experienced prison bureaucrat becomes a realist, however, if nothing else. In most correctional facilities, classification is the most important function contributing to the effective operation of the institution, and staff members with such responsibilities can wield significant influence behind the scenes. Performed properly, classification can ensure a safe, well-run facility; on the other hand, a shoddy process can lead to disaster.

By the late fall of 1972, Parchman's classification committee had gained considerable clout. Although the body owed its existence to federal judge William Keady, that fact alone served to solidify its newfound influence within Parchman's clannish bureaucracy.

Membership on the committee included involvement in decisions that affected every stage of an inmate's incarcerative career, not to mention the direct impact such decisions had on prison operations. Camp assignments, parole recommendations, disciplinary actions, work and school assignments—all had to be approved by the members. Every request to make an inmate a trusty, canteen worker, or houseboy, or to make any other sensitive assignment, had to be brought before the classification committee. From the inmates' perspective, there was another function of the committee that overshadowed everything else: making furlough recommendations. Each year, between November and February, Parchman released several hundred inmates on ten-day Christmas furloughs. It was a practice that had begun in the 1940s, as a reward for hard work and good behavior. The classification committee was responsible for screening the prison population and recommending to the warden who should be thus rewarded. As one might expect, the five committee members were lobbied constantly by inmates and staff alike.

Thanks in large measure to the partnership I had forged with Tom Graf, my stock continued to rise steadily with John Collier. I had taken my classification duties seriously, performing well enough for the warden to demonstrate his confidence by designating me as the committee's vice-chairman, thus permitting me to gain even more influence with other members of his administration.

I knew only too well, though, that my bureaucratic advance could just as easily crash without warning. Mississippi's unwritten rules of politics dictated that those most closely aligned with Parchman's warden were usually among the first to lose their jobs when administrations changed. The harsh realities of the political spoils system at Parchman hardly concerned me, however, in the fall of 1972. After stumbling from one job-threatening crisis to another in my early months there, I enjoyed basking in John Collier's confidence and influence. Though I could in no way lay claim to membership in the warden's inner circle, my appointment to the classification committee and elevation to vice-chairman ensured that I was no longer treated as an outcast. In some respects, I was rather amused by it all. Even though I knew that many administrators regarded me with greater distrust and suspicion than ever, circumstances dictated that, for the time being at least and however begrudgingly, they had to admit me partway into their bureaucratic club.

Graf continued to serve as the real conduit between me and Collier. If my friend were suddenly to fall from grace, I knew that the extent of my true influence with the warden would quickly be revealed. In the meantime, I was determined to make the best use of the limited influence that I did have. Even then, however, I sometimes found myself at odds with Collier or other members of his administration, endangering the fragile credibility I had fought so hard to gain. Nevertheless, I considered it infinitely more important to safeguard the integrity of the classification process than to be politically or bureaucratically correct all the time.

One case of conflict grew out of a violent confrontation between two inmates one evening. The dispute began over some clean bed linens. Walter "Deadman" Lee, a trusty shooter in Camp Eleven, had accused another convict of taking some clean sheets off his bunk. Although this was not the kind of issue that the average man would be willing to kill over, life inside the penitentiary is cheap, and men will kill over far less. In the case of Walter Lee, the other inmate would have been well advised to avoid the conflict—his nickname was apt. Serving a life sentence for murdering his wife, this aging, tall, slender convict had been a trusty shooter for many years. He was known to be quick-tempered and quick with the trigger, oftentimes firing his rifle in the direction of any prisoner who dared to threaten him in any way. Inmate rumormongers had credited Lee with killing numerous convicts over the years, though such claims were greatly exaggerated.

On this evening, Lee was in no mood to be hassled, having worked all day in the fields under a scorching sun. But the other fellow, already courting disaster, upped the ante when he pulled a shank on the agitated Lee. Tiring of the dispute and incensed that another convict would dare threaten him with a knife, Deadman grabbed his rifle and shot the inmate, killing him instantly.

After a brief investigation, officials decided that no charges would be filed against Walter Lee, since the victim had provoked the fight and then threatened him with a knife. Consequently, the administration requested the classification committee to reinstate the inmate as a shooter. Despite heavy lobbying from the warden, and even though the prisoner had been cleared in the investigation, the committee was unanimous in its opposition to placing a rifle back in Walter Lee's hands. He was, instead, referred to Tom Graf for a thorough psychological exam. The administration was not happy with the classification committee's decision, and, as vice-chairman, I was targeted for much of the blame. Fortunately, Graf's report clearly supported the committee's position—not only did the inmate suffer from a significant personality disorder but his I.Q. tested in the severely retarded range. Such convincing evidence appeared to carry little weight with certain members of the administration, however. Although I was confident that we had made the proper decision, I was also painfully aware that the controversy had resulted in some very bruised egos within the John Collier administration, and that I was largely to blame.

Such was the stuff of everyday life at Parchman in that long year of 1972. It was, in many respects, a painful time of change for an institution that was searching for identity in the midst of scandal. A symbol of "old guard" Mississippi politics, the penitentiary vigorously resisted efforts to bring it into the latter half of the twentieth century. For the administration, it was a long and arduous journey, but one from which the federal courts would permit no turning back. For the inmates, however, it was a different kind of journey—a journey of hope.

As the days passed, and autumn began slowly to give way to winter, I had become thoroughly (and happily) involved with my new duties in classification. At long last, I had actually begun to carve my own comfortable niche at Parchman, and in corrections. There was as yet no hint that my remaining time at the penitentiary would soon draw to an eventful close. As I was pulling my red and blue state pickup into the driveway one evening, the radio dispatcher alerted all units that shots had been reported in the vicinity of Camp Eleven. Since my promotion to case manager, life had all but become routine for me. On this fall afternoon, however, I would be jolted back to reality by a stark reminder of just how nonsensical the idea of any prison "routine" can be. Negotiating the sharp curve in front of the First Offenders' Unit, I sped toward Camp Eight, just visible in the distance, leaving a long trail of dust and gravel flying behind me. As I continued on toward Camp Nine, the dispatcher broadcast another message. The shots had been reported in the vicinity of the sergeant's house, adjacent to Camp Eleven.

A hundred different scenarios began to fill my imagination. The possibility of prison employees and their families being injured, or even killed, by convicts was an ever-present danger at Parchman. Inmates carried guns and were allowed to work as "houseboys" at staff members' residences—a system that courted disaster. On the other hand, the report might be nothing. Employees often hunted on the twenty thousand acres of prison land, and sergeants frequently permitted their trusty shooters to do the same—unsupervised.

As I quickly passed the Reception and Classification Unit at Camp Nine, Camp Eleven came into view. From a distance nothing seemed out of the ordinary. The sergeant in charge of Camp Eleven was a good supervisor—even-tempered with a very quiet disposition, not exactly the sort of man one would guess had retired after nearly a quarter of a century in the marines. Suddenly, I realized that I was on top of the sergeant's house, which rested just a few yards back on the right side of the road. As I slammed on the brakes, the truck careened off the gravel and skidded to a sharp stop in the small front yard that bordered the house. Snatching the microphone, I frantically notified the security dispatcher of my arrival at the residence. In the distance, I could see swirling clouds of dust as a line of vehicles rapidly approached from the direction of Camp Seven. For the time being, however, I was on my own, or so I thought. I had not noticed the security van parked by the side of the house.

Unable to detect any activity coming from the residence, I cautiously stepped from the truck. Reaching under the front seat, I retrieved the loaded pistol that was still assigned to me. At that moment, I bolted upright as I heard the front door of the house swing open. An inmate, whom I immediately recognized as the sergeant's houseboy, stepped hesitantly onto the front porch. George Scales (commonly known as "King") was a stocky black man in his early twenties. There was nothing particularly remarkable about him as prisoners went. One of ten children, he came from the nearby Delta town of Sledge. Scales had been sentenced to Parchman in 1969 under a life term for the murder of a grocery store owner.

Although he had already been imprisoned for four years, he did not bear many of the usual trappings of incarceration, such as jailhouse tattoos or disfiguring scars. Polite and deferential, as all Parchman trusties were expected to be, he was a very quiet sort who rarely smiled, and then only reluctantly. Generally he was pleasant enough to deal with, although conversing with him could be tedious and painfully drawn out. It was also sometimes difficult to understand him because he mumbled so much and seldom made eye contact while speaking. His gait was halting as well, and I could not recall ever seeing him in a hurry. In short, Scales was what Tom Graf politely referred to as "slow." But, slow or not, he was in Parchman for a brutal slaying, and I was not taking any chances.

The sight of the inmate visibly shaking made me stiffen. Shielding myself with the door of my pickup, I called out to him, asking if anything was wrong, if there had been some trouble. It was obvious that something was amiss. The sergeant's state truck was in the driveway, along with his wife's automobile, yet there was no sign of them or of their two preschool-aged children. Scales had not moved off the porch, but he suddenly began wailing and sobbing, sending shivers down my back. I did not know what I would find inside the house, but my imagination was running wild. Although praying that the family was unharmed, instinctively I knew otherwise. The convict had his hands hidden from view behind his back.

Slowly I stepped from behind the truck door and nervously trained the pistol on the inmate who stood at the top of the porch steps. I did not like what I was thinking, or what I saw. When I shouted for Scales to put his hands on top of his head, he began wailing in nearly hysterical tones. I screamed my order at him as loudly as I could several more times in rapid succession, but to no avail. The inmate was not making any overtly threatening moves, just rocking back and forth, from side to side, with his hands held behind his back. It was difficult to tell who was more frightened, Scales or me. I would venture a step or two from behind the truck door, then quickly take refuge again. Finally, out of utter exasperation (and no small amount of fear), I barked at the convict to put his hands on his head "before I blow the damned thing off."

Then he began repeating, slowly, over and over, "I didn't mean to kill him, I didn't mean to kill him." The awful reality of what he was saying put me in a state of near panic. One last time, I screamed for him to walk down the steps slowly and lie face down. His eyes wild, Scales finally began to descend the porch steps, his legs wobbling uncontrollably. He had still not moved his hands from behind his back, so I cocked the pistol, ready to use it at the slightest hint of danger. Motionless, I stood a few steps in front of the truck, hollering repeatedly for him to get his hands on top of his head. Although unable to see a gun or any other weapon, I simply had no way of knowing what he might have concealed inside his shirt or trousers, or behind his back.

Without warning, two officers burst through the front door, one furiously shoving the inmate down the rest of the steps, where he tumbled to the ground. Only then did I realize that the prisoner had been handcuffed the whole time. Both men were highly agitated, shouting at Scales, telling him they were going to kill him. I all but leaped to where the convict was lying, grabbing one of the officers by the arm and asking what the hell was wrong. Pulling away from me, he ran back up the porch steps, screaming that the sergeant was dead. I took several deep breaths in rapid succession, trying to calm myself, but my stomach felt as if it had just taken a blow from a heavyweight prizefighter. I did not want to believe the two officers, but I had heard Scales's admission with my own ears. Reaching down, I tugged on the sobbing inmate's arm, roughly jerking him to his feet. The hair on the back of his head was matted with blood, still oozing from a deep gash in his scalp. When I asked the convict how he got hurt, he said the officers had beaten him with a pistol.

As other officers were streaming out of their vehicles along the gravel road, I turned and looked Scales in the face, standing toe to toe with him. "Where are Maxine and the children?" I asked in a deceptively calm voice. The inmate, still crying and shaking violently, insisted that he had not harmed them.

There had been no time yet for me to enter the house, so I was unaware that Amos Meeks's body was sprawled on the floor, just inside the front door. Several other officers were running toward me, but I anxiously told them to check the house for the sergeant's wife and children. One of them asked about Meeks, and I numbly replied that I thought he was dead. Just a second or two later, someone yelled from inside that the sergeant had been killed. He had apparently been shot with his own revolver, and was found in a pool of blood on the living room floor.

Gripping Scales's arm tightly, I could feel his whole body trembling (as was my own). The place was soon overrun with security personnel and front-office brass. The officer who had discovered the body, the same one who had shoved the convict down the steps moments earlier, slowly staggered out the front door, shouting and cursing. As I turned to ask Scales the inevitable "Why?" I briefly glimpsed Warden Collier entering the house. I suddenly and violently jerked on

Just a few yards from Camp Eleven, Sergeant Amos Meeks was gunned down in his home by inmate George Scales.

the inmate's handcuffs again as I growled for him to start walking to my truck. A lot of people, highly emotional and agitated, were milling around outside the house, making a tense situation even worse. A group of four or five officers approached, loudly cursing and shouting racial epithets. The man who had shoved Scales down the front steps was especially rowdy and enraged, which came as no great surprise, considering his reputation among the staff as an obnoxious loud-mouth. I realized that things were quickly getting even more ugly.

Deciding to take no chances, I removed one of the convict's hands from the restraints and hurriedly handcuffed him to me; this seemed to infuriate the enraged officer even more. Calling me a "nigger lover," he screamed for me to let Scales go—"give the nigger a chance to run." No one was more angry about the unexpected tragedy than I, but I had no desire to be party to a lynching. Trying to calm the officer, I asked if he knew anything about the sergeant's wife and children. They were okay, he responded bitterly, that is, if I considered a white woman being raped by a nigger convict okay. Scales blurted out that he did not do anything to her, but I pulled sharply on the handcuffs that joined us together and told him to shut up. The inmate needed to be moved, and soon, to solitary confinement in the death row unit.

The officer came back again, spewing more of his venom, egging his colleagues on. I looked around the ugly, chaotic scene in hopes of finding help, but no one seemed to be in charge; the warden and other administrators were all still inside. As the officers continued their ver-bal taunts, exhorting me to let the prisoner run, still others began to join in, angrily jabbing the inmate with riot batons while shouting words of hatred that were not reserved for Scales alone. I had always been soft on convicts, they hissed; I was a "nigger lover" too, they guessed, since I had seen fit to handcuff myself to the inmate. Scales kept frantically muttering "please, please" as the officers positioned themselves in a semicircle before us. By then, I had slowly backed the inmate and myself against the pickup.

Having managed to secure a host of other officers to support him, the bellicose leader of the group became louder and more animated. He carried his slender build with an exaggerated swagger, matched only by his endless braggadocio—a little man trying to be much larger than he really was. Often the butt of jokes and snide comments among other employees, on this autumn afternoon, he was in his element, strutting around like a banty rooster. Much like a convict, he preferred to put on his best performances before an interested audience.

Repeatedly he baited Scales with taunts and threats, to the derisive laughter and jeers of others who were watching. Standing almost nose to nose with the inmate, the officer pleaded mockingly for me to let Scales go. "Nigger, I'll count to ten before I shoot," he taunted repeatedly. George Scales could only stare at the ground as the officer angrily screamed for him to look at him. The inmate inched closer, his trembling body all but leaning on me as he shook his head and cried out that he would not run. One of the camp sergeants then stepped up to Scales and put his arm around the sweating inmate, giving him an exaggerated hug. Quietly, I briefly pleaded with him: "C'mon, sarge, let it go." Glaring at me with hate-filled eyes, he declared matter-of-factly, "Boys, what we need he'uh is a happening." At that, the officer who had been leading the verbal assault on Scales stepped back and removed his sunglasses—ever so slowly, relishing the drama of the moment. Without warning, he poked the convict in the abdomen with a riot baton, looking at me and smiling as he did so. "No, sarge, he ain't gonna run," he said spitefully, "cause his daddy here," nodding vigorously at me, "won't let him."

I reached to grab the baton, noticing as I did so that Tom Graf and John Collier were coming out the front door of the house. The officer angrily jerked the baton from my grip, again telling Scales to run. Much to my relief, Collier and Graf were walking in my direction. Shoving my way past the angry circle of officers with my prisoner in tow, I stopped and turned around. Moving forward, I got up in the face of the obnoxious leader of the group—so close that it was impossible not to smell the odor of his chewing tobacco. His lips were parted only slightly, revealing yellow-stained teeth clenched in anger; his face was flushed, and I noticed the blue veins straining against the sides of his neck. Staring defiantly into the officer's dark eyes, I addressed the inmate barely above a whisper. "Don't do it, George. Don't run. The bastard will cheat. He won't mean to, but he will, 'cause he can't count to ten!" For a split second the officer was speechless; then his face became blood-red with rage as he promised that I would be sorry. Finally someone else in the group pulled on his shoulder, urging him to ignore me.

I backed away slowly, savoring the combination of confusion and rage that registered on his face. Then I heard Tom Graf's distinctive laugh behind me, and he put his arm around my shoulder. He had witnessed my exchange with the officer a few seconds before. "Jesus, Donnie," he chuckled sarcastically, "cut his nuts off, why don't you?" Giving me a strong slap on the back, he whispered that the angry crowd would love to get hold of Scales. (Tom had overheard much of the angry rhetoric that had been circulating among the riled spectators.) When John Collier finally spoke, he simply inquired in a very subdued manner if everything was all right. In view of the tragedy that had occurred that afternoon, my response must have seemed inappropriate to some—I smilingly held my arm aloft so he could see that Scales was securely handcuffed to me. Hands on hips, the warden's large frame shook as he laughed and nodded approval. When he directed Graf and me to put Scales in the back of his car for transporting to the death row unit, I breathed a sigh of relief. There would be no lynchings that day. After everything that had gone on, the ride to death row was anticlimactic, taking little more than five minutes. For George Scales, however, it was one early step in a long ordeal.

I returned to my house later that evening to find my wife and son sitting forlornly on the front porch, suitcases packed. The murder of Amos Meeks had been the final straw for Miriam. Our existence at Parchman had hardly been idyllic. The house never had received even so much as a fresh coat of paint, much less major renovation. The mice continued to overrun the house, and a hundred squawking turkeys overran the yard. Miriam spent most days curled up in a recliner, our son in her lap. She was afraid to walk around the house, knowing that whenever she did, mice would scurry in all directions.

The word of Amos Meeks's murder had spread rapidly throughout the institution. Stepping from the truck and slowly approaching the front steps, I could readily see that Miriam had had enough of Parchman. "Please, let's go to my mama's house. I can't stay here another night." That was the abrupt conclusion to our living at Parchman.

Later that night I lay in bed, unable to sleep, as the afternoon's events played themselves over and over in my mind. I could not help wondering what had driven Scales (seemingly docile enough) to erupt in a sudden, unexpected, violent rage. What had possessed him to murder Amos Meeks? Perhaps it was not really unexpected at all. The inmate was doing time for a brutal killing, hacking a shop owner with a meat cleaver. I shook my head in the darkness, convinced that Scales probably should have never been permitted to work as a houseboy.

The prison environment is fragile, and violence among inmates can occur without warning, lacking rhyme or reason. Prisoners kill each other over the most trivial issues—trivial, at least, to the outside world. But convicts do not normally minimize the killing of a prison guard; even they are more circumspect than that. There has to be a motive, an unusual, compelling reason for an inmate to murder a prison employee. Scales's sobbing protestations kept coming back to me— "I didn't mean to kill him." My mind ran through all sorts of scenarios. What if it was not a case at all of *what* made George Scales kill Sergeant Meeks? Maybe, just maybe, it was a matter of *who* prodded him to murder. Even as I finally started to drift off into a fitful sleep, I reminded myself not to let my imagination get away from me. But there had been disquieting rumors, ugly prison gossip that hinted at trouble in the Meeks household.

When a prison employee dies in the line of duty, the entire staff is soberly reminded of just how tenuous life can be. The next morning, feeling like I had not slept at all, I apprehensively walked down the unusually quiet hallways of the administration building. Clearly the staff was in mourning, with people clustered here and there, speaking in hushed tones. Eye contact was difficult, if not downright painful. For a brief time, Amos Meeks's death would bring the staff together, forging an emotional bond in an otherwise hostile, unforgiving environment.

Not surprisingly, I was the object of some jaundiced stares and unflattering comments that morning. Preventing George Scales from being severely beaten, or even killed, did not win me any friends. Yet I felt nothing but empathy for the staff. They were entitled to their anger and resentment. What they did not know, could not understand, was that I was hurting too. I had worked with Amos Meeks on the security force. I knew him and got along well with him. Standing in front of his house, realizing the awfulness of what had happened, I too wanted to hurt Scales, to do to him what he had done to Amos. But I could not take my own personal vengeance as justice. I had been scared out of my wits by the angry little mob that had become so ugly. I had even considered the possibility of just leaving—letting Scales fend for himself. I had wanted to get as far away from there as I could, but I had not been able to bring myself to do that either. I had finally done the only thing I could do, and I awoke the next morning knowing it had been the right decision.

Slowly making my way down to the records office, I was almost relieved at the interruption of my thoughts caused by the sound of John Collier's voice calling me. Quickly closing the door without a word, the weary looking warden sank into his swivel chair, sighing loudly. Nervously drumming his fingers on the desk, he looked up and expressed his gratitude for the way I had handled myself the previous evening. My eyes drifted away from Collier's intense gaze. I wanted to tell him how I really felt, how I, too, had wanted to hurt Amos Meeks's killer. I started to speak after a long silence, but was interrupted by an insightful Collier. "Everybody was mad as hell yesterday. We all were. But we're supposed to be better than the convicts, and if that boy had gotten hurt yesterday, we'd been no different than him."

Nodding in agreement, I started to take my leave, but was forcefully commanded to sit back down. Without mincing words, John Collier leaned forward, his huge hands clasped together, and asked me what I thought had "really" happened the day before. I could not possibly know what had "really" happened, but I assured the warden that all was not as it seemed.

The sergeant's murder proved to be the beginning of the end for John Collier as warden. Under intense media and legislative pressure, Governor Bill Waller appointed a special commission to investigate Parchman's inmate houseboy system. Headed by a highly respected circuit judge, J. C. Feduccia, the inquiry was exhaustive and agonizing. The same could not be said of the investigation of Amos Meeks's death. George Scales was convicted, of murder, in Sunflower County

Circuit Court and sentenced to serve a second life sentence. Many troubling questions about the case remained unanswered. Scales admitted to killing the sergeant, but he implicated Maxine Meeks as the moving force behind the crime. The convict painted a picture of a cold, shrewd, calculating woman who wanted her husband dead so that she could collect his life insurance money. Allegedly, Maxine Meeks talked Scales, whom she had supposedly been having sex with, into killing her husband; in return (by the convict's account), she promised to send ten thousand dollars to Scales's family. Although she failed a polygraph test concerning her involvement in the murder, the investigation never led to an indictment of Maxine Meeks. Soon after testifying at the trial, she left Mississippi, never to be heard from again, but reportedly financially secure.

Following the completion of the Feduccia inquiry, which recommended ending the use of inmates as household servants, Collier's administration quickly began to unravel. Within a matter of weeks, Tom Graf decided to leave Parchman; soon after, John Collier was also gone. With Tom, my closest friend and ally, already out of the picture, John Collier's demise as warden meant the end was in sight for me, though it would not come immediately. His replacement never succeeded in gaining confidence from or credibility with the staff. Rife with suspicion verging on paranoia, the administration was doomed from the beginning. The new warden sought to rid himself of anyone suspected of being a Collier loyalist, and I fit the description perfectly. Not coincidentally, I provided him with the perfect excuse for firing me.

Parchman had a rather well written inmate newspaper, *The Inside World*, that was published monthly. Jimmy Johnson, one of the inmate editors, had asked me to write a guest editorial. I was hesitant at first, but Johnson (known as "the professor" because of his master's degree in English from Columbia University) prevailed upon me to comment on the many unsettling changes that had followed John Collier's departure. The editorial was highly critical of the new administration. While I did not attack the idea of change itself, I roundly criticized the air of uncertainty and instability that had been fostered by the new warden. Foolishly, I believed he would actually accept my comments in the spirit in which they were offered—constructive criticism!

Before running the presses, the employee in charge of the penitentiary print shop brought the editorial to the warden's attention. I was summoned later that night and ordered to clear my desk and be off the prison grounds by the next morning. Fortunately, I was not caught completely by surprise—I already had a job waiting for me as a parole officer. I left without argument and with no real regrets. It had been a stormy year, and in a way I was relieved that it was over. But as I went through Parchman's front gate early the next morning, I vowed that I would return again one day—as the warden.

Twelve years later I kept my promise, taking the reins on October 1, 1984. It was humbling to return to the scene of so many personal trials and pains that had severely tested me early in my career. On my first night on the grounds as warden, I went out of my way to find George Scales. Ironically, he was now a canteen worker in the old First Offender's Camp, site of my first assignment at Parchman many years before. I did not know if he would remember me, or even want to see me, but I very much wanted to see him.

Entering the camp, I was flooded with a rush of memories and emotions. George Scales appeared from behind the canteen door, walking slowly across the bare concrete of the dining room floor. For a moment neither of us spoke. He looked older, and heavier than I remembered, but then I had lost a little hair and gained more than a few pounds myself. I could not help smiling, a silent acknowledgment that neither of us was a youngster anymore. I held out my hand and George's face lit up. Tearfully embracing me, he whispered, "Old friend."

The sound of the cell door sliding open reverberated up and down the death row cellblock, jolting me back to the present. Connie Evans was lying on his bunk watching television. As he sat up and swung his stockinged feet around to the floor, he grinned and quietly greeted me with a handshake. As I sat down on the end of the bunk I looked intently at the young man before me. For a brief moment, I silently pondered the vow I had made so many years before. I had kept my promise to return to Parchman, but I wondered now for what purpose. Diligently I reminded myself that I was an instrument of the legal system, "just doing my job." Thinking I had known, for all the years I had been a prison administrator, what corrections was really about, I found myself besieged by a growing uncertainty.

Distracted by my thoughts, I slowly became aware that Evans was good-naturedly chiding me for disturbing his "morning rest." Looking around the small, neatly arranged cell, I dropped my head and stared at the floor. Cutting Connie off in midsentence, I mumbled that an execution date was about to be set. He was stunned by my unexpected announcement, sitting speechless and motionless for a very long time. Finally he stood up slowly, exhaling deeply as he grasped the bars on the cell door. I watched as he looked up and down the cellblock, as if already contemplating his final walk to the death house.

For the next couple of hours I remained in his cell, our conversation coming in small spurts until it was clear that we had both run out of things to say. Preparing to leave his cell, I patted him on the back, offering a few words of encouragement. Though it sounded unconvincing, even to me, I insisted that there was still time.

As I quickly stepped through the sliding cell door, eager to get out, he hollered after me, almost matter-of-factly, "Hey, no there ain't." Connie was right, and we both knew it. He had returned to his bunk, nervously rapping his fingers on the metal bed. Staring at the floor, he remarked wistfully, "I've always known this day was coming, but who believes, Warden, who really believes?"

Approaching Fury

Putting men to death in cold blood by human law seems to me
a most pernicious and brutalizing practice.

Horace Greeley, 1872

Codified law has existed in various guises since the emergence of the
earliest clans. Humankind, throughout its history, has attempted to
pursue justice in numerous conceptions and forms. Of course, justice
as Americans know it today is the result of centuries of experimentation and refinement. It is the outgrowth of an evolutionary process that
constantly requires revision and fine-tuning. Before rudimentary forms
of government emerged, justice was imposed on a very personal level,
with retribution as its focus. Although one of the most misunderstood
concepts in modern jurisprudence, retribution is still an important
component of contemporary American justice. This is particularly the
case in the controversy about capital punishment. Ironically, the notion of retribution is supported by both those who seek to abolish the
death penalty and those who staunchly defend it. The abolitionist sees
retribution as a way to limit inhumane punishment; the defender of
capital punishment embraces it as a viable way to end the coddling of
violent criminals.

Caught between these competing forces is that great indefinable
mass called the "public." Even though Americans pride themselves on
being a humane and compassionate people, as in any reasonable society there are defined limits as to what the public is willing to tolerate.
As the twentieth century ends, it appears that popular sentiment is

shifting significantly—support in the United States for the increased use of the death penalty may be at an all-time high.

Whatever else Americans may sense about capital punishment, the specter of the execution chamber reminds us of our darkest, most disturbing frailties as individuals and as a society. No other topic seems to grip the public's consciousness in quite the same manner. It is a highly charged debate, with both sides prone to histrionics and sentimentalism, and ordinary citizens are frequently left confused and angry by the contesting parties. Americans despair of a criminal justice system that is unresponsive to their needs, and death row prisoners represent a criminal justice process gone awry. It seems to the ordinary citizen that criminals possess more resources and more rights than law-abiding people. That a murderer can slay his victim without warning, and then pursue years of legal appeals from a death row cell, is particularly galling to the public. With a force and volatility characteristic of few other issues, the question of capital punishment haunts the American psyche, arousing almost universal curiosity and engendering forceful expression of opinion from even the most temperate of bystanders.

For me, however, as I bade farewell to Parchman in 1973, executions were hardly of any real concern. The United States Supreme Court had, just a year earlier in *Furman v. Georgia*, decided that existing death penalty laws violated the Constitution. True enough, the justices had not ruled that capital punishment was a form of cruel and unusual punishment, as the abolitionists had hoped (except for two justices, William Brennan and Thurgood Marshall, who considered executions unconstitutional under any circumstances). The Court did, however, assail the manner in which death sentences were dispensed. In spite of this partial victory for the abolitionist forces, the justices left the door ajar for states to devise new statutes that could meet Supreme Court scrutiny. The willingness of the Court to reconsider capital punishment laws notwithstanding, the future did not appear particularly auspicious for death penalty supporters, among whom I definitely numbered myself. Given the justices' five-to-four vote in the case, many more questions necessarily remained open than had been answered. What is more, there had been an unofficial moratorium on executions since 1967, and, as yet, there was no real groundswell of public support for resuming them. All in all, it was not difficult to presume in the summer of 1973 that executions in the United States were relics of the past.

Other matters were more important to me at the time, however. Although leaving Parchman was bittersweet, I was determined not to give in to a sense of having been defeated. I had a career to build, and over the next five years I set about gaining as much hands-on experience as possible. I wanted to make myself a "marketable commodity," someone who could eventually compete for any corrections position in the country. So, from 1973 to 1978, I took on a series of progressively more responsible jobs that exposed me to many different facets of Mississippi's slowly evolving corrections system. Working as a parole agent for adults, juvenile probation officer, and director of the state's first restitution program, I had the good fortune to pick up a well-rounded view of corrections.

During those same years, Connie Ray Evans was unwittingly moving toward catastrophe. In 1973 he was still just a thirteen-year-old in junior high, although he was beginning to evidence the restlessness typical among children of that age. Bored and feeling confined in school, he was already an "at risk" youth who wandered aimlessly about Jackson, Mississippi. Evans found the lure of the streets irresistible, a welcome relief from the restraints imposed by growing up in a large family in a poverty-stricken black neighborhood. Although he had never known his biological father, he seemed to get along well enough with his stepfather most of the time. But between holding down jobs and caring for the other children, neither his mother nor stepfather was able to afford him the supervision and individual attention he increasingly needed. By Evans's own admission his parents tried, but they could not compete with the combination of bad company and the fast life that attracted him to the streets. Before long he encountered his first minor difficulties with the law. Still, as he approached his fourteenth birthday, there was nothing serious enough to enable one to predict the magnitude of the tragedy that awaited him. Somewhat ironically, prison, though far removed from the youngster's mind, was not completely unknown to him. An older brother (an unsuccessful petty criminal) had done time. Still, the gangling thirteen-year-old could not have possibly conceived of what awaited him in Parchman Penitentiary's gas chamber.

Just as my career underwent many changes in the mid-1970s, so did Mississippi's prison system. In 1976 the state legislature, in a rare demonstration of courage and progressive thinking, passed a bill that created the Mississippi Department of Corrections. It was no small legislative achievement, considering the many obstacles that had to be overcome. Reform-minded legislators had dreamed for many years of creating such an agency, but their efforts had always been stymied by the more conservative elements ruling the legislature.

Parchman Penitentiary, for three-quarters of a century, *was* corrections in Mississippi. Established by the legislature in 1900, the institution replaced the notorious and scandal-ridden convict-leasing system. Post-Confederate Mississippi was a land ravaged by battle, literally penniless by war's end. The first prison in the state had been constructed in Jackson in 1846, on the site of what is now the Old State Capitol. It was a typical walled institution, with cellblocks and tiers that kept inmates securely confined. During the Civil War, the prison was used as a munitions plant; although the facility remained standing while General Sherman burned Jackson to the ground, it suffered extensive damage. With the end of hostilities, the legislature decided the state could neither afford to renovate the prison nor pay for the upkeep of prisoners, and the old building was demolished. Thus began the era of convict leasing, one of the most infamous chapters in the history of American penology.

In fairness to the Mississippi legislature, the leasing of convicts must have seemed a logical solution at the time. The state, after all, faced dire circumstances. Those few plantation owners and well-to-do farmers whose land and homes were not totally destroyed in the war had no labor force—the slaves had been freed. Using convicted criminals as agricultural laborers seemed to be the only viable alternative. Unfortunately, greedy businessmen and unscrupulous politicians ensured that the system would fail. In consequence, the state was saddled with an embarrassing reputation for inhumaneness and brutality in the treatment of its convicted criminals that would persist well into the latter half of this century.

After much prodding from an increasingly critical press, the legislature abolished the convict-leasing system; for the first time in nearly four decades, a new state prison was established. Not by accident, the institution was located in The Delta. In 1900, Mississippi was still very much an agrarian society, as was most of the South. The legislature initially purchased some fifteen thousand acres of farmland in Sunflower County (a later transaction added approximately seven thousand more acres). It was the intent of both the legislators and a parade of governors that Parchman be a self-sufficient institution. The penitentiary, named after the first warden, J. M. "Jim" Parchman, was ideally located in the midst of the fertile Delta lands. The growing season is long, and, given adequate resources and labor, farming can be bountiful. With a dependable supply of convict workers there was nothing to prevent the prison farm from flourishing. Indeed, for the sixty years after its opening in 1901, the State of Mississippi would benefit mightily from the sweat and toil of Parchman's convicts. They raised vegetables, pork, poultry, and beef, feeding not only themselves but juvenile offenders in the state training schools and patients at the state mental hospital. Moreover, Parchman's dairy herd provided ample supplies of fresh milk, butter, and cheese.

And then there was the cotton—thousands of acres of it, stretching as far as the eye could see. Parchman developed a reputation for raising some of the finest stands of cotton in the entire Delta. It was meticulously tended by hundreds of convicts who spent long, backbreaking hours in the fields until every last scrap was harvested. The considerable profits from the operation, however, went directly to the state's general fund—the penitentiary failed to benefit in any perceptible way.

While developing its reputation as a model of efficiency, the prison farm also became the subject of occasional speculation about the brutal and dehumanizing treatment dealt out to inmates. For the most part, neither state officials nor the public particularly cared how prisoners were treated at Parchman. Most people probably did not even know where it was, and they liked it fine that way. Besides, the inmates were supposed to work, and prison was not to be an easy experience. Many people reasoned that if it took an occasional whipping to get a convict to do right, then so be it. Corporal punishment assumed a significant role in Parchman's everyday routine. An infamous leather strap, "Black Annie," became the most feared instrument at the farm. Two or three feet long and about six inches wide, the strap was a quarter-inch-thick piece of cowhide that could lay open a man's back and make his flesh raw. Tales abounded among inmates and staff alike concerning Black Annie's victims over the years.

As a young guard at Parchman, I was reminded of the strap's painful effectiveness by an old convict. He had been at the penitentiary for years, serving life for stabbing a man to death, and in his younger days he had been whipped with Black Annie many times. Then he realized one day that no matter how hard the sergeant laid the strap across his back he no longer felt anything. Slowly peeling his shirt off, the old man turned around, revealing a back grotesquely scarred by the repeated beatings. The nerve endings in his back had been so damaged that he could no longer sense pain, but he had been wise enough to keep on hollering and screaming, begging for relief each time he was whipped. If he had not, he reasoned, the sergeant would have just found some other part of his body to whip. Black Annie was not outlawed by the Mississippi legislature until the late 1960s, and there were many who believed such action to be a terrible mistake.

Many legislators from districts that included or lay close to Parchman wanted very much to maintain the status quo. Throughout its existence, the prison farm had been a rich source of political patronage. This fact was not lost on The Delta's political barons, who strenuously opposed any effort to create a statewide corrections agency. A department headquartered in Jackson, rather than at Parchman, would surely mean less power for those legislators who had come to regard the penitentiary as their own personal property.

Supporters of the corrections bill were determined, however, to break the back of political interference in Parchman's affairs. The only way to do that was to create a department of corrections and make the Mississippi State Penitentiary subordinate to it. Curiously, among the leaders in the effort was a young member of the state house of representatives, R. G. "Bunky" Huggins. That his own district lay within Parchman's long shadow was no small tribute to his political courage in taking the stand that he did. But Huggins was, in fact, just one of a number of young turks in the legislature who parted ways with their other Delta colleagues. Representative Ed Jackson and Senators Bill Alexander and Howard Dyer were among those who risked political suicide by supporting the corrections department legislation. It was Bunky Huggins, however, who perhaps had the most to lose, since he was a key member of the House Penitentiary Committee. Under that body's rules it would have been quite simple for Huggins to kill any legislation that proposed creating a corrections department. Instead, he openly supported and campaigned for the concept, which proved crucial to the bill's finally becoming law.

If Huggins's support for the corrections legislation was crucial, Senator J. C. "Con" Maloney's involvement was indispensable. The senator, from Jackson, had no personal dog in the fight as far as Parchman was concerned. But, as chairman of the Senate Corrections Committee, Maloney had seen more than enough to convince him that the only way to curb the corruption and abuses at Parchman was to create an agency that would have oversight responsibilities. The senator provided the real impetus for the legislature to act when he introduced the bill that would create a corrections department. Although its backers hailed it as a significant breakthrough in the state's prison history, they could not have foreseen the political treachery that lay ahead for Mississippi's newest state agency.

Tyler Fletcher rendered perhaps the most courageous leadership of all. A polished, highly knowledgable criminal justice professional, he had left the army after a distinguished career. As a civilian, Fletcher single-handedly established a program at the University of Southern Mississippi for educating police officers. Appointed by the governor to the thankless job of chairman of the State Penitentiary Board, Fletcher put his prestige on the line in the fight to establish and organize Mississippi's first Department of Corrections.

Throughout the wrangling that preceded final approval of the bill, Governor Cliff Finch largely distanced himself from the battle, but he quickly signed the measure into law upon passage. To the surprise of many experienced political observers, Finch brought in an outsider to be the new department's first commissioner. Ellis MacDougall was a veteran corrections administrator, one of the biggest names in the field; he carried impressive credentials, having served successful stints as commissioner of corrections in both South Carolina and Georgia. MacDougall had a reputation as a progressive penologist, a trouble-shooter who enjoyed tackling difficult problems. He possessed as well a certain flamboyance, accented by his distinguished middle-aged good looks. Since Cliff Finch was viewed by some as the epitome of good ol' boy politics as usual, his appointment of MacDougall was a puzzlement. Perhaps it was the penologist's flashy approach that attracted him, for the governor was rather adept at showmanship himself. To gain his surprise electoral victory, he had run a superbly orchestrated campaign designed to appeal to Mississippi's working-class voters. Criss-crossing the state with a black lunchbox in hand, Finch "worked" at various jobs, creating the illusion that he was cut from the same cloth as ordinary Mississippians. Each day of the campaign, citizens were treated to a steady diet of newspaper photographs and nightly newsclips of the gubernatorial candidate—shirtsleeves rolled up and looking resplendent in blue jeans instead of the three-piece suit in which he usually practiced law. One day he might be sacking groceries in a country store; the next, he might be tack welding at a shipyard on the Mississippi coast. Although Finch was known as an accomplished political showman, even the governor's detractors had to credit him for appointing a savvy prison administrator, one with strong credentials, to boot. Finch had pulled another rabbit out of his hat full of tricks.

Ellis MacDougall quickly made it clear that he had come to Mississippi only long enough to get the new corrections department up and running. Despite the short-term nature of his plans, the new administrator's presence was still reassuring. MacDougall's personal reputation was well deserved, but his track record for selecting and developing other successful managers was equally impressive—this was what had brought stability and continuity to the agencies he served. After an impressive performance as South Carolina's prison chief, MacDougall moved on to Georgia, leaving his former responsibilities in the hands of an impressive young administrator, Bill Leeke. Leeke went on to serve as commissioner of corrections in South Carolina for nearly two decades. A few years later, when leaving Georgia, Ellis MacDougall once again waved his magic wand and produced another bright understudy, Dr. Allen Ault.

In many respects, Finch's appointment of MacDougall had seemed to ensure a rebirth for the state prison system. Thanks to the wise leadership of Con Maloney, Bunky Huggins, and others in the legislature, the bill that Governor Finch signed into law was a model piece of legislation. And it was not only designed to end decades of political arm-twisting at Parchman—it was also meant to depoliticize the state parole board. Historically, members of the parole board had always been appointed by the governor. Con Maloney's bill did not seek to change the appointment process, but it did attempt to end the political patronage that had been associated with the board. Parole officers, the agents in the field who actually supervised adults on probation or parole, were hired and fired by the board's chairman. Until passage of the corrections bill in 1976, such work did not provide much job security. Officers served strictly at the will and pleasure of the board chairman or of the circuit judge in whose district they worked. Circuit judges wield tremendous influence in Mississippi politics, and they had become accustomed to having a great deal to say about who was appointed to a parole position, and for how long.

The political patronage of the old parole board was far flung, and the networking of the good ol' boy system effectively influenced most of its hiring decisions. Senator Con Maloney, however, finally (and shrewdly) reined in much of the parole board's patronage power. Under the 1976 act, the board would no longer concern itself with the hiring and firing of officers; it would be responsible only for granting paroles. Field agents were to become part of Mississippi's personnel system, subject to the same practices in hiring, promotions, and terminations as other state employees. Maloney's bill had set the wheels of progress in motion, and many optimists (myself included) expected the new agency to be a success.

Leaving Parchman in 1973, I felt scarred and embittered by the political storms that had constantly buffeted the prison; by 1976, however, I was convinced that Governor Finch and the legislature had taken significant steps to cure the penitentiary of its political ills.

Others, more experienced than I in Mississippi politics, were not so optimistic.

True to his word, Commissioner Ellis MacDougall announced his resignation from the new department of corrections just six months after his arrival in Mississippi. I was grateful to him for bringing me back to the adult corrections system. After completing the requirements for a master's degree at the University of Southern Mississippi, I had gone to work with the state's Department of Youth Services as a juvenile probation officer. It was a grueling job, with few more successes than what I had witnessed in adult corrections. Although I learned a great deal during those eighteen months, I never grew really comfortable in the position—it takes a very special person to work with troubled kids, and I was not one of them. My heart was, and always would remain, in working with grown-ups. So I felt "rescued" when Ellis enticed me back to adult corrections. My enthusiasm and optimism renewed, I eagerly seized the opportunity.

Although the news of MacDougall's impending departure was no surprise, the announcement of his replacement stunned everyone. Dr. Allen Ault had been persuaded to give up his secure position as commissioner of Georgia's corrections department to come to Mississippi. A MacDougall protégé, Ault was one of the most highly respected men in corrections. Those of us who labored in Mississippi's still embryonic agency were clueless as to how MacDougall or the governor had induced Ault to leave Georgia, but it did not matter. Elation swept over the Department of Corrections, as well as the progressives in the legislature. So vibrant was his personality, so sure was he of his abilities, that Ault made everyone around him feel confident. The future did indeed look bright, at long last, for Mississippi corrections. Yet, even as Ault took command, the bubble was soon to burst with stunning swiftness—he would serve as Mississippi's corrections chief for barely six months, resigning abruptly to accept a similar job in Colorado.

There had been rumors of turmoil and discontent at the department's highest levels, but rank-and-file employees were largely unaffected by it all. Allegedly, Finch and his political cronies were trying to dictate hirings and firings to Ault. Allen was a strong, independent-minded bureaucrat, and a pragmatist. He understood, better than most, the necessity of crafting compromise in the political arena. There were certain principles, however, on which he would not yield. While resisting attempted intrusions into his agency's territory, he thought (mistakenly) that he had a good understanding with the governor. The end came one morning when he received a list of names—names of corrections department employees to be fired. Although the reasons for the governor's displeasure were not clear, very often such decisions had almost nothing to do with job performance and everything to do with politics. Ault refused to comply with Finch's demand, opting to leave for greener pastures. Of course, the governor tried to put the best face possible on the whole thing, but he had created a monster that quickly escaped his control, igniting the wrath of many legislators and members of the press. But it was the Department of Corrections that came out the biggest loser. Sadly, Mississippi had lost the services of one of the brightest, most capable leaders in corrections. For the next four years, the state's correctional system once again reverted to politics as usual.

In 1978, I decided to leave for a job in Florida. I had enjoyed my association with the many dedicated people who worked so hard, with so little support, in Mississippi's correctional system. Had I been content with the status quo I probably could have remained indefinitely, but I felt that it was time to move on. Neither the legislature nor the governor was inclined to entrust the system to professionals. The constant bickering and political manipulation following Allen Ault's resignation rendered the department all but impotent—it was drifting, without purpose or goals.

Florida's correctional system offered a thoroughgoing contrast. My appointment as chief administrator of a small institution in Gainesville presented an exciting opportunity to prove myself as a manager, something I had been striving for since leaving Parchman five years earlier. In many ways, I could not have selected a better place to go: Florida's correctional system was held in high regard; and once again, almost as if by design, I would benefit from the personal guidance and friendship of an experienced administrator. Louie Wainwright, the near legendary director of Florida's extensive prison system, became (like Charlie Gaughan in Massachusetts) a mentor who was influential

in shaping my career from then on. Wainwright did not cut an imposing physical appearance. His short, stocky frame was accented by salt-
and-pepper hair, and he sported a pair of bifocals on his smallish face.
Always well dressed, he possessed an engaging personality, with a
quick wit and ready smile. More importantly, he had earned a reputation as a very able corrections administrator, one who had worked his
way from corrections officer to head of the agency.

Wainwright was quite adept at trench warfare, whether doing
battle with convicts or politicians. For nearly a quarter century, he
ruled the nation's fourth largest correctional bureaucracy, turning aside
every attempt to unseat him. Even his most bitter adversaries grudg-
ingly acknowledged that Wainwright's long tenure had brought uncommon stability and continuity to the state's prison system.

My years in Florida were largely uneventful, though certainly not
unimportant. It was a time to learn and grow, to gain respect and credibility in the rough-and-tumble world of prison administration. It was
in Florida that, for the first time in my career, capital punishment made
its presence known, even if but peripherally. Executions were once
again approved by the Supreme Court in 1976, slowly gaining renewed
acceptance in the country's scheme of justice. The Court had ruled that
the death penalty could be used, provided it was employed fairly and
impartially. States quickly began to pass new statutes designed to meet
the Supreme Court's requirements, and Florida joined the increasing
ranks of those seeking to end the moratorium on executions.

In spite of the renewed interest in capital punishment, there was
speculation in some quarters that executions were still many years
away; yet within a year of the Court's decision there were signs that
this view was overly optimistic. Utah became the first state to put a
convict to death under the new guidelines when Gary Gilmore was
shot by a firing squad in 1977. Strangely, that highly publicized death
still failed to convince significant numbers of correctional professionals that capital punishment was really back on center stage. (The execution was considered an aberration by many, myself among them.)
Gilmore had, after all, ordered his family and attorneys to discontinue
any further legal appeals, telling Utah officials that he wanted to be

executed as soon as possible. The state obligingly granted his final wish.

Within a year of the Utah execution, however, notice was served on condemned inmates across the land that the death penalty states meant business. Florida was poised to carry out its first execution in more than a decade. Although John Spinkelink was not a particularly noteworthy death row prisoner, his scheduled execution drew scores of media representatives from around the world. Camped out in a field across from the Florida State Prison in Starke, the media had come to witness a new era in America's two-hundred-year-old debate on capital punishment. Unlike Gary Gilmore, John Spinkelink sought to exhaust every possible legal remedy at his disposal. In the end, though, "Old Sparky," Florida's aptly named electric chair, won.

Spinkelink was vastly different from Gilmore. While the latter reveled in (and helped create) the circus environment surrounding his execution, Spinkelink's shy, retiring manner seemed inconsistent with the persona expected of a condemned killer. He possessed neither the manipulative charm of Florida's Ted Bundy nor the demonic charisma of California's Charles Manson. Many who knew John Spinkelink had no doubt that others on the row were more deserving of a date with the chair. Law, however, is not so discriminating. The simple truth was that John Spinkelink had simply been on death row a long time—long enough to have finally run out of legal arguments.

The truth of Spinkelink's impending death never pierced more deeply than in the last few hours preceding the execution. Three of my prisoners happened to be awaiting transfer to death row, having only recently been convicted of the brutal murder of a local businessman. They were typical jailhouse braggarts—easily incensed by anyone, guard or convict, who was not duly impressed by their criminal exploits. All fancied themselves as tough-guy gangster types, yet they were cowards to a man.

It was almost amusing to watch the three killers change as another man's execution approached. All but overwhelmed by the power of the approaching deadline, none of them could sleep or eat; pacing nervously in their cells like caged animals, the prisoners' usual inces-

sant laughter and chatter gave way to scowls. They had been antago-
nistic and threatening toward guards and inmates alike, constant management problems even when confined in isolation cells. But in the
final hours before Florida's first execution in more than a decade, a
heavy dose of reality landed on many a prisoner. The three self-styled
desperadoes discovered that even they were not immune to fear. At
the core of inmates' time in any prison, life is a constant struggle of evil
wills in mortal combat, barely more than an existence. So it was with
these three, especially as John Spinkelink's life neared its end—they
fought their demons alone, with neither keepers nor fellow inmates offering comfort or consolation.

During those last hours—another man's hours—the three of them
had become sullen, irritable, and, yes, introspective. One would have
thought it was they who faced the angel of death. They had been dis-
believing at first, making off-color jokes about another man's date with
the executioner. Then the reality of it all began to squeeze their emotions like a vise. The guards watched silently through the night, detached, taking each man's true measure—the three toughs were now
showing their real feelings before all the prison world.

If the guards had been affronted by what they had seen and heard
from the trio over the months, they mostly kept it to themselves.
Other inmates, however, who had also been subjected to seemingly
endless bragging and delusionary claims of importance, were far less
circumspect in their response. There is a strange code of ethics, even a
sense of honor, among prisoners. The joint is a harsh place, unforgiving of weakness and error. When reality finally set in, when palms
began to sweat, when pleading looks of fear and confusion replaced
buffoonery, the three inmates found no sympathetic ears, only the
stony silence of uncaring brother convicts.

For these three, and for many other condemned prisoners, dawn's
light brought a sobering hour of truth. Yet it was not only the inmates
who were suddenly forced to confront the new reality. For the first
time in my career, I found myself thinking about the "what-ifs." Like
so many others in my profession, I had shrugged off the Gary Gilmore
case a year earlier. That had been different—seemingly less a real exe-

cution than a state-sanctioned suicide. The reality of Florida's first execution in years, however, quickly seized my attention. Others would
follow, and soon the crowds of reporters and film crews, curiosity
seekers and demonstrators would begin to dissipate. After a while,
officials at the Florida State Prison would carry out their grim task with
barely a notice, but there could no longer be any doubt that capital
punishment was back. Even then, I somehow knew that I would one
day execute another human being.

As John Spinkelink died in Florida's electric chair, Connie Ray
Evans was moving closer to Mississippi's gas chamber. Having only recently dropped out of Jim Hill High School in Jackson, the eighteen-
year-old was hurtling toward disaster. He had spent little time in the
classroom during the previous two years (failing two grades), prefer-
ring the living laboratory of street life. An increasing share of his time
was devoted to finding ways to support his experimentation with co-
caine and marijuana. The die was cast, and soon a bitter, street-smart
youth would explode in senseless violence. Our paths moved closer,
but first I would be exposed to another state's death house.

In 1981, an offer of more money and greater responsibility led me
to Missouri. My three years' service there, while not involving any executions, did bring several close encounters with the state's archaic gas
chamber. The Missouri State Penitentiary, in Jefferson City, is an imposing structure, whose high walls hold some of the state's toughest
felons. The oldest penitentiary west of the Mississippi River, it has
housed the likes of Pretty Boy Floyd and James Earl Ray. With sixteen
guard towers looming above twenty-foot walls, rising up within view
of the Missouri River, the penitentiary is a striking architectural feature
of the capital city.

Life inside Missouri's maximum security prison (referred to by locals as "the Walls") was anything but dull—it was a tough joint to do
time in, for both inmates and staff. Missouri had at least a dozen prisons, but the Walls was something special. The atmosphere inside left
little room for indecision or weakness. Violence was an ever present
danger, as rival inmate gangs jockeyed for control of prison rackets. It
was the toughest correctional environment I had ever worked in, both

physically and emotionally. Because of the environment and the constant danger, I grew to have more respect and admiration for the officers who worked inside the Walls than for any other prison staffers I was ever associated with.

It was my kind of joint, the epitome of the "big house." I had always found working in corrections to be exciting and challenging, but there was something exhilarating about being in a maximum security prison. Working at the Walls was like working in Massachusetts again: buildings full of cellblocks four tiers high, chain-link fence extending from ceiling to floor (to prevent inmates from throwing each other or, worse yet, officers to the concrete below), steel bars, and solid walls. Full of tough guys and snitches, punks and thieves, it was a microcosm of the most unsavory aspects of the human race; the sights and sounds and odors left little room for doubt that it was a maximum security prison in every sense of the word. Life was harsher and cheaper in the Missouri State Penitentiary than in any other institution with which I had ever been associated, but, in a twisted irony, that is what made it all the more special. If you worked in the Walls and did your craft well, you knew that you, too, were special.

Once again, I was fortunate to benefit from the counsel of experienced colleagues, whose wisdom and common sense had long contributed to the successful operation of the penitentiary. Donald Wyrick had been there for his entire thirty years in corrections, beginning as a guard and working his way up to warden. After a decade in the warden's office, he had been promoted to deputy director of the Missouri Department of Corrections. Wyrick's knowledge of the Walls was unrivaled. He was a hardworking administrator, an "old school" warden who believed in running his institution with a firm hand. The inmates viewed him with respect and fear, a necessary mix in any maximum security prison. Wyrick was a maverick, the survivor of many bruising battles in Missouri's political arena. He had his detractors, some of the most vociferous being within the corrections system itself. But he was a master tactician, well versed in the art of survival. Governors came and went, corrections directors came and went, but Wyrick was always there. If there was a valid complaint about him, it was that he was a compulsive micromanager, a control fanatic who found it extremely difficult to entrust subordinates with responsibility and authority.

The man who replaced Wyrick as warden, becoming my immediate supervisor, had an entirely different management style. When Bill Armontrout appointed me his deputy warden, he expected me to know my job, and to do it without a lot of interference from him. Bill's long years of experience at the Walls as Wyrick's understudy made him perfectly suited for the warden's job. He knew how to handle people, a skill he had perfected during an earlier career in the navy. His hearty laugh and keen sense of humor made him immensely popular with the members of the staff, though they also respected his ability to be tough when necessary. Bill's patience and coolness under fire contrasted starkly with Don Wyrick's quick temper and sharp tongue.

By the time I arrived at the Walls, executions were gaining momentum. Missouri had a death penalty and a number of inmates waiting on death row, though it would be several years before the state rejoined the execution ranks. Although I had always considered myself a death penalty supporter, working in the Missouri State Penitentiary further solidified my outlook, at least for a while. One of the things that led me to favor capital punishment was the need to maintain a modicum of law and order inside the joint. When inmates were serving sentences of life or fifty years without parole, I was convinced that they had little to lose by assaulting or killing prison employees.

Events one weekend shook my faith in the deterrent value of capital punishment, however. Late one Friday evening, I was advised that an inmate had been found dead in his cell and was summoned to the prison. The incident occurred in the administrative segregation unit, which was no stranger to prisoner violence; it was our "prison within the prison," housing recalcitrant inmates who were chronic management problems. Not surprisingly, the dead man had been strangled in his sleep by his cellmate. What shocked me was the motive. The murderer had previously been the cellmate of another con who was his homosexual lover. The lover became involved in a dispute that resulted in the killing of still another convict from a rival prison gang; consequently, he was prosecuted for murder and sentenced to death. The brooding inmate responsible for the strangling had decided that the only way he could be reunited with his lover was to murder someone so that he, too, would be put on death row. His strangled cellmate was a totally unsuspecting victim of one of the worst acts of prison depravity I had ever witnessed. I could not help shaking my head in disbelief, wondering how the threat of the death penalty could have failed to deter a senseless prison murder. Perhaps, I thought, it was the fact that no executions had yet occurred in Missouri, leading the inmates to view it as a hollow threat.

At different times, several condemned prisoners waited anxiously for their appeals to be granted. On one occasion, the locally notorious George "Tiny" Mercer seemed to be on the verge of going to the death house. Physically, he was an immense specimen who laughed off any fear of the gas chamber. Tiny's fellow bikers had presented him with a personalized birthday gift one year—a young woman whom they had kidnapped just for the occasion. Eventually Mercer tired of, and murdered, his "present." It became apparent after a while that the Missouri attorney general had his sights set on an execution date for Mercer; he notified Bill Armontrout to have the gas chamber prepared, just in case.

I had not given the whole matter of executions much thought until I paid my first visit to the death house one afternoon. Missouri's gas chamber was homemade, having been constructed by prisoners in the 1930s. Strangely, one of the inmates who helped build it later supposedly committed a murder, confessing that his sole motive was to be put to death in the very chamber he had helped build. As prison lore had it, he was granted his wish.

Examining the chamber, Bill Armontrout and I could see that it was in serious disrepair—we were not at all sure that the thing would even function properly. As we worked, Armontrout pointed out that there was a certain notoriety to the chamber. It was the only one in the country, other than San Quentin's, that had two chairs. The second had been added in the 1950s, specifically for a double execution. Curious to hear more, I pressed Bill for details.

A man and a woman had kidnapped and murdered the seven-year-old child of a wealthy Kansas City businessman. On the night of the execution, the condemned prisoners were brought into the chamber together. As the man was strapped into the chair, he was crying hysterically and asking for forgiveness. His partner, meanwhile, kept telling him to shut up, cursing him and everyone else in sight. She finally told the warden to get on with it so she would not have to listen to her cohort's "damned whining" !

The machine had caught my attention while Bill was relating the story, and I was impressed by its simplicity and cold efficiency. The witness room itself was not what I had expected. The Hollywood version always portrayed official observers as seated in two neat rows, but in Missouri there was no such reserved seating. Instead, a semicircular cast-iron railing stood inches away from the observation windows. Crowding around the railing, witnesses looked directly into the face of the condemned prisoner as they observed his death.

Because Missouri did not employ an official executioner, the task fell to the warden and his appointed staff. As the deputy warden in charge of security, I was assigned to mix the chemicals and place the cyanide crystals under the chair. The warden, myself, and the other deputy warden would pull the lever to drop the cyanide into the mixture of sulfuric acid and distilled water.

The process sounded pretty routine to me, but only because I had not yet been struck by the enormity of it all. Even though I was not looking forward to the task, I would merely be doing my job. I had no way of knowing then how many times I would hear the phrase "just doing your job" later on in my career. The day was to come when it would ring in my ears until I wanted to scream. But at this point in my life I truly believed that I was prepared to carry out Tiny Mercer's execution. I was too naïve to understand that nothing could really prepare a person for such a task. My only discomfort was that I found myself liking Tiny just a bit.

The task of updating and modernizing Missouri's execution protocol fell to me, and, slowly, I began to sense the seriousness of it all. It had been nearly twenty years since the chamber had last been used, and in all that time few really believed it would ever be used again.

Ultimately, Mercer's appeal was granted, and it would be another three years before he reached the end of his legal arguments. By that time, I had left to assume new duties as warden of the Mississippi State Penitentiary. The execution techniques I had practiced in Missouri would not be put to use until a steamy May night in 1987, when Edward Earl Johnson was put to death in Parchman's gas chamber. Bill Armontrout would be there to watch.

Parchman
Revisited

Society has erected the gallows at the end of the lane
instead of guideposts and direction boards at the beginning.

Bulwer-Lytton

Returning to Parchman in the autumn of 1984 gave me great personal
satisfaction. Driving through the front gate that first day, I noticed a
large, freshly painted sign that warned approaching visitors against
bringing contraband onto prison grounds. At the bottom it read, "Per
Order of Donald A. Cabana, Superintendent" in bright red letters. How
strange it felt, knowing that I had really kept my promise. Who would
have believed that I'd ever come back, let alone as warden? Staring at
the sign, I was momentarily lost in thought, remembering my departure on a hot summer morning in 1973. A highway patrolman escorted
me off the grounds, a final act of humiliation imposed by a nondescript
political appointee who occupied the warden's office. In a gesture of
defiance, I turned to the trooper and bitterly asserted that I would be
back one day. I never allowed myself to forget the sarcastic smile on
his face as he laughed derisively, "Sure you will!" I wondered where
he was: retired probably, maybe even dead. Too bad, I thought, for I
truly wished he could have been there to witness my return.

I had not set foot on the Parchman prison farm in more than a
decade, but I knew there had been many changes, the most significant
of which had been the growth of its population. In 1972, Parchman
housed barely two thousand inmates, but by the time I assumed the
warden's duties some five thousand men called the place home. Yet as

I drove slowly down "Guard Row" I was struck by how little the front end of the institution had changed. The warden's residence looked exactly as I remembered. The "main house," as it was often called by prison employees, was not a particularly imposing structure. It was a large, ranch-style home, its features almost plain. Architecturally, it certainly could not compete with the original warden's residence, a magnificent two-story Victorian mansion built at the turn of the century. The old house had been demolished in the 1940s by order of Warden Marvin Wiggins. True to his reputation as a scrupulous guardian of public finances, Wiggins constructed the new residence out of materials salvaged from the old. The house was still surrounded, though, by majestic oak trees that towered above everything else around them. How graceful they were, standing guard over the many families that had occupied the place in the past eighty years. The lawn and the shrubbery were perfectly tended. On the north side of the house was a tennis court, long since fallen into disrepair; a couple of basketball goals had been placed at either end, but they, too, revealed the ravages of long years of disuse. Laughing aloud, I knew that the old court would come to life again just as soon as my family arrived. They would come within the month, and when they did the genteel tempo that had always seemed to envelop the main house would never be the same. We were a large family, noisy and gregarious, with four healthy children, including a set of twins. But that was not as big as it was going to get—Miriam and I were awaiting the arrival of a second set of twins within a few months!

As I stepped out of my car and slowly walked to the back door of the house to go inside for the first time, I wished so much that my wife could be with me. It was Miriam's moment of victory as well, for she had endured the hills and valleys that a career in corrections imposes. I had moved often to new jobs, cheating both her and our children of any sense of permanency or continuity, yet she never complained. This move was different, though. We were coming back home to Mississippi.

I had never been inside the house before, though I had often tried to imagine what it was like. I was not disappointed in the least, and I knew that the empty house would soon become a home full of love and bustling activity. The den was comfortable and inviting, with a cozy fireplace at one end and a baby grand piano at the other. The dining room beckoned with a round antique table, wonderfully large, that would more than accommodate my growing family. The place was bigger than it looked from the outside, with rooms that were large and airy. Walking through, inspecting each room from floor to ceiling, I could not help thinking of the ramshackle little place that stood next to the turkey pen out by the old First Offender's Unit. It was just a few miles away down a dusty gravel road, but it was part of another world, and I marveled at how far Miriam and I had journeyed. Strolling through the backyard, I noticed a very old pecan tree that shaded the house from the afternoon sun and would provide a ready supply of delicious nuts in the spring.

Standing on the front porch, I gazed at the surroundings for a long time, taking in everything I could. I was truly home, back where I had longed to be for so many years. I almost had to pinch myself to see if it was real. It was rather odd that I should feel this way, for I had spent only a year at Parchman, and then under difficult circumstances. Although my career had since taken me to half a dozen other locations, I had always wanted to come back to Mississippi. To return as Parchman's warden had been a burning ambition for a dozen years (Miriam occasionally thought I was obsessed by the notion); I never allowed myself to forget how I had left the penitentiary. It was not so much that I was fired—it was the humiliation, the derisive manner in which it was all done. I went on to a successful career, but always there was a kind of emptiness that no other job could ever fill.

Across the highway I spied Camp One, which I had not noticed when I first arrived. A living monument to a bygone era at Parchman, it was one of the oldest camps, having been erected by inmate labor with bricks that were manufactured in the prison's own brickyard. Popularized in song by inmates and blues artists (who were sometimes one and the same), Camp One, according to prison legend, served as the basis for the popular song "Midnight Special." Years earlier, a line used by the Illinois Central Railroad ran directly past Parchman, the tracks slicing across the prison entryway. Every other Sunday was visiting day, and the trains stopped to discharge visitors from all over at the front gate. Inmates in Camp One would get up especially early on visiting Sunday, rushing through breakfast so they could clean up and get out to the yard to await the arrival of the first train. There they stood expectantly, knowing that soon their wives and children, parents and siblings would be bringing picnic lunches and cool drinks.

I watched the camp from my front porch, my mind full of memories. I thought also of the prison lore that lay within those old walls. The rail line had long since disappeared, and with it the magic of inmate superstition. Prison folklore had it that the first man who spotted the light of the locomotive when it came by at night would be the next inmate to be paroled. I could almost hear the shouts of joy coming from a chorus of exultant voices. The night train was coming—there it was, off in the distance—and some lucky inmate who had bathed in her light was going home. "Let the Midnight Special / shine her light on me": a haunting refrain about lonely, desperate men in a lonely, desperate place.

The next morning arrived early and I hit the ground running, wanting to squeeze in as much activity as I could. Much of that first day was spent meeting employees and being greeted by department heads. I was inwardly amused by some of the older employees who had been there when I was on the staff. How glad they were to see me, how pleased they were that I was back. Some were sincere, but others were merely playing the game. It was a charade that experienced Parchman employees were quite good at, for it really mattered little to them who the warden or the superintendent was.

The first department head to seek me out, though, was a welcome sight. Tom Bennett had long since left the custody ranks and was in charge of the inmate identification section. Although retaining his wit and keen sense of humor, he had encountered some serious health problems, and it showed: my old boss had lost considerable weight, and his coal black hair was now a distinguished silver. However, when he put his arm around me, telling me how glad he was to see me again, I knew he spoke the truth. Over the next five years, Tom Bennett and I would share many a hearty laugh about our early days together.

That afternoon, I finally managed to escape from my office and began to inspect some of the units. Parchman had indeed changed. In

1972, there were about eighteen camps, most of them small, housing no more than a hundred or so inmates. There were a lot of problems back then, problems that had been allowed to fester by an inattentive legislature. The camps themselves had been run-down, rodent-infested health hazards. Inmates had been routinely brutalized by guards and convict trusties alike. There could have been no question that federal intervention was the only thing that would force the Mississippi legislature to address the crisis at the penitentiary. As I wandered through the various camps that first day, though, it was clear that in the rush to clean up the mess at Parchman the federal court and the legislature had thrown the baby out with the bath water. Among the positive things about the old Parchman had been its size and the configuration of the camps. Unlike many other states, Mississippi in the early 1970s did not yet have a burgeoning prison system; Parchman, the only correctional facility in the state, was still of manageable size. The way the original camps were organized was a prison administrator's dream. A full-scale riot or major disturbance of any kind was unthinkable because inmates had no way to band together in large numbers. The smallness of the camps also permitted a sense of informality that simply did not exist in most correctional facilities. The camp sergeants knew their inmates, and they got to know their families as well.

And, yes, there was the work environment. Inmates worked long, arduous hours in the fields, sometimes under less than acceptable circumstances; but they were not confined inside a cell or dormitory all day, and, most importantly, they were not idle. No prison administrator faces a greater adversary than inmates who have nothing to do. In the Parchman of the early 1970s, all able-bodied inmates worked, and the institution was productive.

What I found during my first days as Parchman's superintendent, however, was profoundly disturbing. The institution had truly been transformed in the last dozen years—to just another prison. Unit Twenty-Nine was a concrete and steel testament to the "new penology" that had swept the place. Somehow it had apparently been decided that in order to improve and modernize the old Parchman, near-total destruction was called for. Although a considerable number of older camps (Front Camp, and Camps One, Four, and Seven) were still in use, no effort had been made to retain the good features of the old order. Not only was Unit Twenty-Nine a concrete monolith surrounded by double fences, razor ribbon, and motion detectors—it housed fifteen hundred inmates. True enough, the physical plant was a vast improvement over the old camps. Inmates at Unit Twenty-Nine were not cooking on wood-burning stoves, nor were they showering ankle deep in raw sewage. Yet, in the rush to modernize, Mississippi had repeated the architectural blunders of other states. Gone was the ability to deal with inmates in manageable groups; gone was the intimacy that developed between camp inmates and staff, between inmates' families and staff. Despite the evils of the old camps, there were also many positive features, but these were lost forever as the old camps were torn down.

Criss-crossing the vast acreage in those first days, I found the fields empty except for an occasional patch of vegetables here and there. Large areas were either overgrown from years of lying fallow or were leased to local farmers for their private use. Missing were the rows of cotton stretching to the horizon; gone were the endless fields of vegetables that would feed inmates year-round. Although the dairy barn was still standing, the herd had long since been auctioned off. Missing were the henhouses and the pens for hogs and turkeys; so too were the slaughterhouse, the canning plant, and the beef herd. I did, however, find yet another new housing unit under construction, the future Unit Thirty. Not quite as bad as Unit Twenty-Nine, it was, nevertheless, another typical prison facility—five hundred dormitory beds, where everyone would become just another faceless entity.

Amazingly, in the midst of all the untilled soil, five thousand inmates lay about with nothing to do. Thousands of acres of land wasting away, miles of ditches overgrown with weeds, Camps that were dirty and littered. It was not the Parchman I had remembered, or the one I expected to inherit. Prisoners no longer farmed, I was told, because it was not cost-effective. How, I puzzled, could it be "cost-effective" to more than double a prison's population and then give the inmates nothing to do? No one understood better than I that there was not much demand on the outside for people who were experienced at picking vegetables or cotton. My initial concern, however, lay not in providing convicts with vocational skills but in getting them out of bed and back to work! It was sheer folly to have five thousand men caged inside dormitories and cells all day with nothing to do but get into trouble. I had not been at Parchman long when I realized that the first major hurdle to be cleared was putting inmates back to work.

I finally got around in the first week to visiting the death row unit. Here, I met Connie Ray Evans for the first time. Strolling down the cell-blocks, I noted that most of the inmates were on their bunks, reading or watching television. How different the environment was from when I had worked there so long ago! The death row unit was one change at Parchman of which I did approve—officers no longer had to wear rain gear and rubber boots just to walk down the tiers!

A few prisoners stirred to see who was on the block, one or two exchanging routine pleasantries. Nearing the end of the tier, I noticed an inmate at a cell door, his gangling arms hanging loosely between the bars. He offered to shake hands, asking if I was the new warden. Nodding affirmatively, I asked him who he was. Almost reticently, he gave me his name, Connie Ray Evans, and said he had been on the row for about four years. I had bidden him farewell and started back toward the other end of the block when he quietly asked if I had a minute. Breaking into a wide grin, I knew he was going to ask for some small favor. Hell, I thought, if I were locked up in an eight-by-ten cell for twenty-three hours a day, I would try asking for anything and everything—especially of a brand new warden! He chuckled softly at seeing me smile, knowing what I was thinking. Nervously rubbing his bare foot on the concrete floor, he hesitantly asked if I would consider allowing men on death row to receive a Christmas package from home. I burst into spontaneous laughter, and he began to laugh, too, mischievously casting his dark brown eyes toward the floor. I was not making fun of him, or of his request. Rather, it was a bit of prison humor that inmates and wardens understood, even if no one else did—it was the swiftness with which he made the request that had made me laugh. "Damn," I replied jovially, "you don't waste much time, do you?" Raising both arms above his head to clutch at the steel bars, he chuckled that he was just trying to "break me in" early. I told him I would think about it and let him know, but that he ought to write me a note. As I started toward the door at the end of the cellblock, he hollered, "Hey, sir, just so you don't forget, what's my name?" Without breaking stride, I shouted back, "Evans. Now what's my name?" "Warden," he enthusiastically replied. " 'Warden'—is that good enough? Hey, Warden, don't forget me now!"

As the days turned into weeks, I began to comprehend the enormous challenges facing me. Not the least of these was politics. Of course, that came as no great surprise, since Parchman had been a political football throughout its long history. In recent years, however, it had become more entrenched than ever in the muck and mire of good ol' boy politics. Having considered the penitentiary a prize political trophy in years past, some legislative barons refused to let go of what they had grown to regard as their private political domain.

By 1983 my predecessor in office, Eddie Lucas, had come under increasingly hostile criticism from certain elements in the legislature. Berating the prison administration for lack of leadership, legislators kept up a continuous assault on Parchman. Most prison administrators are required to endure such politically motivated accusations from time to time. Administering a correctional facility is one of the more professionally difficult jobs in government service, and, because wardens are often political appointees, change is inevitable. Mississippi had suffered, for decades, from instability and lack of managerial continuity in its prison system. Since 1855, only five wardens had managed to survive the rigors of running the state's penitentiary for longer than four years. It was no great surprise, then, that by 1983 Eddie Lucas was traveling a bumpy road as Parchman's warden. Though it appeared that a move might be afoot to replace him, in Mississippi's political arena nothing is quite what it seems. Even among those who clamored for change, there seemed to be little agreement as to how they might engineer such a move.

The Mississippi Board of Corrections, a five-member group of gubernatorial appointees, was the governing authority for the Department of Corrections. Although the board appointed the commissioner of corrections to manage the department's everyday operations, key administrative appointments and terminations had to be submitted to the full panel. The warden's position at Parchman was most assuredly considered a top administrative post. Legislative critics could make all the noise they wanted, but only the board and the corrections commissioner could implement a change in Parchman's leadership; not even the governor was empowered to intervene directly. The warden, however maligned by legislative critics, could not be dislodged easily. Moreover, this situation required careful handling by critics, for Eddie Lucas was the first African American to serve as warden; as such, he was one of the highest ranking blacks in state government. Whatever Mississippi's racial past had been, the political realities of 1983 were far different—African Americans constituted an increasingly formidable force at the ballot box and in the state's house and senate.

One thing that can honestly be said of Mississippi politics: if a situation in state government presents itself as a problem, the executive branch will undoubtedly make it worse; if the legislature becomes involved, however, the problem will become a nightmare! From the earliest days of Parchman's existence, a succession of governors and legislative bodies had made prison politics into an art form. Virtually every warden had, at one time or another, felt the long arm of the legislature, and Eddie Lucas was no exception. Even though he did not personally merit much of the criticism concerning the penitentiary's operation (the warden's sins were not so much those of substance as those of style), he was held accountable nonetheless.

I had known Eddie for many years; he had come to work at Parchman shortly before I left. A massive man, with jowls framing his large face, Eddie had hands that any politician would be proud of—large, with a viselike grip. A man of many moods, he could change disposition quickly, almost unpredictably. While he enjoyed a joke, and his own sense of humor was genuine and infectious, he could often seem impersonal, even cold. One could hardly mistake his anger, however. His deep, resonant voice would rise to a crescendo, filling a room with booming utterances that were both humorous and deprecatory.

When the 1984 legislature went into session, a rather ingenious plan evolved to deal with the Parchman problem. There was no longer a question of whether the prison was to have a change of leadership, but when and how the change would occur. Yet the most vexing issue was *who* would control the penitentiary. Parchman certainly had some significant problems, but much of the trouble was beyond the immediate influence of the warden, or even of the corrections commissioner. That official, Morris Thigpen, a professional administrator of proven ability and unquestioned integrity, was held in high regard by a large segment of the legislature. Yet, like Lucas, he was subjected to a barrage of scathing criticism by a handful of fierce legislative opponents. In the main, they did not like the corrections commissioner because he refused to play their brand of politics, resisting repeated attempts to crown Parchman as the dominating power broker in the state correctional system.

Rather than confront the unpleasantness of forcing Eddie Lucas out of office, the legislators chose the path of least resistance. They simply created a new position, correctional superintendent, to supersede that of warden; hence, the task of dispatching Lucas would fall to the new superintendent. It was a perfect solution, at least from the legislature's point of view. That august body could boast of having addressed the leadership issue at Parchman, while avoiding a nasty political clash over Lucas's dismissal.

In any event, although I was personally grateful for the opportunity to return to the penitentiary, I was also a realist. I knew only too well that I would not enjoy a long tenure as superintendent—a few years would be the best I could hope for, given the political climate. One of the most unpleasant prospects that confronted me as soon as I took the reins was what to do about the warden's position. I moved quickly, convinced that Parchman had no need for both a warden and a superintendent: within the first two weeks, I appointed Eddie Lucas director of inmate classification. His knowledge and expertise in that area were extremely valuable, and he would prove to be a tremendous asset to my administration.

Once on the scene it did not take long for me to recognize the magnitude of difficulties faced by the head man at Parchman, no matter what his job description. Anyone who aspires to such heights in the corrections business had better realize early on that his true friends will be few and far between. I certainly never lacked for people who posed as friends, employees who were full of suggestions. Many were merely self-serving bureaucrats, placing their own interests ahead of the institution's. (That was, after all, how business had been conducted at Parchman since anyone could remember.) For many of the veteran employees, there was no real commitment or loyalty to the prison administration, only lip service. Most prison staff, however, were conscientious, dedicated people who soldiered on under the most difficult circumstances.

Politics was the machine that drove Parchman. While a warden or superintendent was trying to mold the penitentiary into a responsive, efficient operation, others were busy pursuing different agendas. Some legislators never hesitated to involve themselves in what should have been the exclusive domain of prison administrators. From the hiring and firing of employees to what shifts officers would work, certain gentlemen from Jackson made it their business to lean on the administration at every twist and turn. It was the single most frustrating aspect of the job that I encountered. Much like the prison administrator who cultivates inmate "snitches," some legislators groomed employees to function as informants on the administration. A legislator told me one day that there was nothing I could discuss in the privacy of my own office that he would not come to know about later. Then he humorously asserted that I should not take it personally, that every warden at Parchman had been required to tolerate such a system. Sadly, I knew what he said to be true.

Working in such an environment tends to color one's perception of the world—after a while, one becomes suspicious of everyone and trusts almost no one. It was my good fortune, however, to be blessed with a true "best friend" at Parchman. Wayne Fleming had been there a long time, starting as a sergeant at the old prison hospital. A genuinely decent human being who was universally liked and respected by the staff and the inmates, Wayne possessed the innate abilities of a leader, yet was humble enough to never forget his roots. I had always been fond of him—I suppose more than anything else because he had been good to me when I was just a young, naïve officer. He was one of the most nonjudgmental people I had ever met, tolerant of all sorts of viewpoints even if he did not agree with them. When I was running around Parchman in 1972 and 1973 like a one-man crusade, Wayne treated me as much with civility and kindness as others did with contempt and hostility. Of medium height and rather stocky, he looked like he could be tough as hell; underneath, however, was a quiet man who kept his job in perspective and concentrated most of his efforts on being a loving husband and father.

I was pleased to discover upon returning to Parchman that Wayne's abilities had not been overlooked, for he had moved up to the rank of colonel. During my first year as superintendent, I gained a great appreciation of Wayne's administrative abilities, as well as his loyalty and friendship. Eventually, I promoted him to deputy superintendent, thereby incurring the wrath of all the deputy wardens who had previously outranked him. Nevertheless, it proved to be the best decision I ever made. I never had to worry about leaving the prison under his command, nor did I have to be concerned about his motives, professional or otherwise. I grew to depend on Wayne extensively, especially when it came to dealing with personnel issues, since he was such a great "people" person. In our few years of working together we had only one serious disagreement—I became angry and hurt because Wayne had decided to leave. Selfishly, I wanted my trusted ally and closest friend to stay, but circumstances just did not permit it. Even though I knew that, his decision made me angry and resentful, though not for long.

Frequently, prisons operate under the rules of "crisis management," and Parchman certainly had its share of crises. In fact, if not confronted with a predicament of one kind or another just about every day, I would begin to wonder if something was wrong. It did not have to be anything major, and often as not inmates were not the source of the problem (although we certainly had our share of those troubles, too). Like everything else, inmate-related problems seemed to go in cycles, with everything running smoothly and then, all of a sudden, the whole place seemed headed for hell in a handbasket. But for the most part, in the spring of 1985, I was satisfied that things were slowly beginning to improve. Some significant changes in the ranks of middle management, especially in the security staff, had brought about new attitudes. The inmates were more disciplined, the housing units were cleaner, and the prison grounds looked a hundred percent better.

The biggest change, however, was the creation of an intensive work program for inmates. For the first time in ten years, the penitentiary planted a cotton crop. Prisoners were once again organized into work crews, and they spent the long spring and summer days tilling the fields. At harvest time, almost everything, including the cotton, was picked by hand. An average of a thousand inmates a day worked the fields, with results that were both immediate and impressive. Behavior improved dramatically, and once again the convicts were productively involved in contributing to their own welfare. For the most part the staff seemed supportive of the work program, although a few officers were vehemently opposed to it. At first, the inmates tested my resolve, but as soon as they understood that they were going to work, voluntarily or otherwise, most of them accepted their new role and did what they had to do.

However, on one particular morning the inmates were unusually contentious, with work squads "bucking" (engaging in work strikes) everywhere. The prisoners had been picking butter beans for several days and had apparently grown weary, so they sat down in the rows and refused to move. It began with just a dozen or so, and then quickly spread until most of the crews were involved. I tried reasoning with them, since I knew that picking butter beans was not much fun; the plants grow quite low to the ground, necessitating a lot of bending over, which can be grueling work. After failing to reach an accommodation with the inmates, I ran out of patience with one group that was taunting the officers and otherwise being rowdy. I instructed the major in charge of field operations to fire a few warning shots over the prisoners' heads to get their attention. For a while, the tactic seemed to have worked—the men scrambled everywhere and started picking beans as if they were possessed. However, that afternoon the inmates began bucking again, complaining that it was too hot, their shoes were too tight, and so on.

Before I arrived at Parchman, the standard practice had been to take striking inmates from the fields and return them to the camps to be placed in lockdown. That, in my opinion, was precisely what they wanted. So on the day of the great butter bean strike I ordered them all shackled, and they remained in the fields until the regular workday was over. Any who wished to change their minds and return to work were permitted to do so without further penalty. The convicts were also told that they would be transported to the fields the next morning, right on schedule at 6:30; those who refused to work would again be shackled. Clearly, the confrontation was becoming a test of wills. The next morning, dozens of inmates, without shoes or socks on their feet, lined up at the waiting flatbed trailers for transportation. There had been a rash of inmate "thievery" during the night—a fairly good tactical move on their part, I thought. The prisoners were convinced that no reasonable person would make them work in the fields in their bare feet. However, I was in no mood to be either reasonable or conciliatory. Ordering the officers to take them to the fields, with or without shoes, I did not care if one bean was picked that day. One thing was certain, however—the inmates would be there, shackled, all day if necessary, bare feet and all!

Because they had escalated the confrontation another notch by not wearing footgear, I decided not to transport them to work on the flatbeds. Instead, the officers walked them to the fields. It was not an easy trek, nor was it a short one; more than a mile of asphalt, rapidly absorbing the midsummer heat, awaited them, followed by a long stretch of gravel road. They had not traveled more than a few hundred yards before some of them began capitulating. Inmates who agreed to return to work were taken back to the camp to retrieve their shoes and socks; those who did not continued their trek to the fields. I also raised the stakes further, promising each of those who held out that I would immediately stop deducting "good time" from their sentences. Good time is simply a number of days that is subtracted from a prisoner's sentence for good behavior, and it is a powerful disciplinary tool for a warden. When the procedure is suspended, an inmate, in effect, has time added onto his sentence. I broadened my threat with a promise to those who were eligible for parole, telling them I would place a negative recommendation in their file for every day that they refused to work.

A few of the strikers were serving mandatory sentences, however, which meant they were not eligible for either good time or parole. In their case, I imposed sanctions on visitation, canteen, recreation, and other privileges. By the end of the second day, all but four of the original several hundred strikers had decided to return to work.

Following that incident, we never really had any other major problems with inmates bucking. Of course, there were always those few "tough nuts" who were recalcitrant as hell. Most of the other cons did not want to be around them, lest everyone suffer the consequences. The majority of prisoners just wanted to do their time and get back home as quickly as possible, and a lot of them actually preferred working to sitting around and doing nothing. One old con who proclaimed the virtues of the work program put it succinctly: "By the time these boys work all day in the fields, they're too tired to fight and fuck at night. It's got so a fella can actually get some sleep up in them camps now."

Unfortunately, other confrontations with inmates did not end quite so peacefully. During one stretch of summer months, the staff endured a nasty series of events that tested the limits of our patience and luck. Over eight weeks, Parchman had half a dozen hostage incidents. Although none resulted in serious injuries to employees or inmates, nothing worries a prison administrator more than a group of marauding convicts who are holding prison employees hostage. One incident in particular nearly ended in disaster. Unit Twenty-Two had been a hot spot all that spring and summer. Several stabbings had occurred within a few days of each other, and the tension in the unit was noticeable to officers and inmates alike. Then a confrontation erupted in which several inmates threatened to assault correctional officers, chasing them out of the dormitory with brandished knives. I ordered the unit placed on lockdown until I was convinced that things had cooled off. The lockdown was lifted after a week, but within twenty-four hours I would regret my decision.

I was driving around the farm the next morning when the dispatcher notified all units that officers had reportedly been taken hostage in Unit Twenty-Two. As I was just a short distance away, I drove directly to the site, and went inside immediately. The so-called experts always insist that during any major crisis the warden should be in his or her office, safely removed from the impending threat. The warden, after all, must call the shots, which is difficult if he is being held hostage. So I violated the first principle of good management by going to the scene personally, and compounded my error by entering the unit without waiting for the arrival of other personnel; but I knew (hoped!) that they would be right behind me.

Once inside the dayroom, I found five convicts holding guards at knifepoint. An argument had apparently erupted in the dining hall over the confiscation of an inmate's radio. Without warning, the prisoners overpowered the officers, taking their keys and cutting the telephone lines. Luckily, one guard managed to run to the case manager's office, locking himself in and reporting the incident from a telephone in the office.

There had been little time to evaluate the ramifications of being in the middle of a confrontation with knife-wielding convicts. Cautiously walking across the dayroom, I ordered the inmates to drop their weapons and let the officers go. One of them flashed a toothless grin and sarcastically asked if I was going to disarm them all by myself. Not an unreasonable question, but one I did not wish to ponder when I was standing there by myself. I realized then that I had probably just committed myself to being taken hostage as well; assessing the situation, I suddenly felt very uncomfortable. Relief arrived, though, in the person of a large contingent of officers. My anxiety level quickly climbed again, however, as Col. Barry Parker whispered that all the doors to the dormitories were unlocked. Just what I needed to hear—two hundred more inmates could join the festivities at any second. Taking my eyes off the hostages for a moment, I scanned the dormitories. The inmates were all sitting on their bunks, their attention riveted on the events in the dayroom; none of them had made any overt moves, and I hoped that they wanted no part in the confrontation. Barry moved quickly to lock all the dormitory doors, eliminating, without incident, one possibly very severe complication.

Even though I should not have been in the unit, the incident had happened so quickly that everybody, including the inmates, was caught somewhat by surprise. In fact, since I was already there, nothing was to be gained by leaving; such a move on my part could have led to a rapid deterioration in the whole affair, which I wanted to avoid at all costs. My primary concern at that moment was to get the officers out unharmed.

It had not required much effort to figure out who the ringleader was. As I had looked at each inmate, one clearly emerged as the spokesperson. All the inmates involved were black, except for one white boy—the leader of the group. In those first moments, I repeatedly instructed them to surrender their weapons and let the officers go, but none of the prisoners spoke or made any overt moves. Except for the white convict, who was extremely agitated, the inmates seemed relatively calm. The incident appeared to have been spontaneous, because the hostage takers obviously had no plan; in fact, they did not even express any demands, other than making very general complaints about the officers being "unfair." The problem with most prison hostage situations is their unpredictability. Some can be resolved very quickly, and without violence, while others may drag on for days, and still end in bloodshed. This one was no exception.

As the minutes ticked by, I gradually arrived at a strategy. There were a number of crucial factors to consider. Even though we had managed to get the dormitories locked down and secure, all the inmates could still see and hear everything that was going on. The longer the hostage takers were permitted to control things, the more we risked other inmates being tempted to engage in riotous behavior, and I did not need two hundred other cons tearing up the dormitories, setting fires, and generally creating additional problems for us to cope with. My primary goal remained constant: to defuse the situation, getting the officers and the inmates out unharmed. As long as other prisoners did not become involved, I was convinced the odds were on our side. A large force of officers had assembled in the dayroom. In spite of issuing strict orders that no one on the security force was to make any overt attempt to engage the hostage takers, I was prepared to take any action necessary, including the use of lethal force, to free the hostages. Still talking with the hostage takers, trying to buy time until I could decide upon a final course of action, I knew only too well that the situation could deteriorate almost without warning. It was imperative to find a way to end the standoff as quickly as possible, without jeopardizing the officers' lives.

In observing each of the inmates, I had concluded that their spokesman also happened to be their weakest link. Of grave concern, however, was the fact that he also appeared to be the most unstable of the group. The boy reminded me a great deal of another inmate I had confronted many years before, in the First Offender's Unit, the North Carolinian who had tried to run. I was convinced that the situation could be resolved peacefully only if I managed to break the hostage takers' ranks, turning them against each other.

Directing more and more of my attention to the other four inmates, I sought to drive a wedge between them and their young ringleader. Constantly reassuring them that I did not want anyone to get hurt, I repeatedly asked them to drop their weapons and release the hostages unharmed. For a short while I thought I might be reaching a couple of them. I was absolutely convinced that some of them did not want to be involved—a hopeful sign. The problem in these situations, however, is that even though the inmates may be searching for a way out, they have got to save face. There they were, in front of two hundred other convicts, all staring at them. Capitulation would not come easily.

As their initial emotional high began to subside, a couple of the hostage takers started speaking a bit more reasonably. Then, with absolutely no warning, the young white boy exploded in rage. What I had feared most suddenly seemed to be becoming a reality. Everything was about to unravel unless the boy's emotions were quickly brought back under control. Threatening to kill his hostage on the spot, he tightened his grip on the shank in his hand, sharply jerking the officer's head back with his forearm. Once again, I tried reassuring him of my intentions, but he was no longer in a mood to listen. I had angered him by focusing almost exclusively on the other inmates; they tensed up visibly as the boy screamed a torrent of obscenities at me. Reminding myself to speak calmly but forcefully, I tried to avoid upping the ante if I could help it—five officers' lives hung in the balance! When he paused for an instant, I seized the opportunity, telling him in a soothing tone that no one had to be hurt, and that we would continue to talk as long as necessary.

He venomously attacked the notion that I might be concerned about his safety. His face a fiery red, blue veins straining against the sides of his neck, the boy screamed in a guttural tone, "Fuck you, asshole! You don't give a damn about me or any other convict. It's this damned police you worried for." (Parchman inmates commonly referred to correctional officers as "police.") He was at least partially correct: I was scared as hell that I would not get my officers out alive, especially if I could not get him calmed down. But any thoughts I entertained of reasoning with him evaporated in the next few seconds. In a moment of dangerously high agitation, the inmate lightly, but purposefully, scratched the side of the officer's neck with his homemade knife. I held my breath, sensing a look of horror cross my face. The line had been drawn. Any further discussions would be nothing more than a ploy on my part to buy time; a plan had to be devised, and quickly, that would get as many of the hostages and inmates out alive as possible.

For an instant, I thought that the situation might still be resolved with minimal danger to all concerned, but I quickly rejected the idea. An element of grave risk was involved if I were to incorrectly presume his dramatic gesture to have been just that—a gesture, and nothing more. Looking at him intently, I thought it possible that he really did not intend to kill anyone, but I could gamble no longer. His apparent instability was of increasing concern. Although I could not afford to display any open hostility, his attempt to get my attention by scratching the officer's neck had worked. Inside, I was struggling to control my temper. There would be no turning back, not after his little moment of high drama. I would not walk out of that camp until the hostages had been released and order restored.

Never raising my voice, I moved a step closer, and then another, until I could almost reach out and touch him. Ignoring his warnings that the officers would all be killed, I interrupted him and calmly demanded that he listen to me. I struggled to present a deliberative, even cold, demeanor; it was as critical for the hostages, and for the staff who were gathered behind me, to believe that I was cool and relaxed under fire as it was for the hostage takers. The ringleader was jerking the officer's head back again. He said nothing, but he moved the shank up and down the side of the hostage's neck, grinning as he did so. We were in a staring contest, our eyes fiercely locked, each looking for any sign of weakness in the other. If I did not make him blink, I thought, someone was going to die. With every bit of cold-bloodedness that I could summon up, I reached behind me, touched whoever was standing there, and said, "Get me a shotgun."

The boy was bothered by huge beads of perspiration rolling into his eyes. Angered anew that I had called for a weapon, he pressed the shank against the officer's throat harder, signaling no retreat on his part. I could hear one of the other convicts mutter that they needed to "give it up." The ringleader quickly told him to shut up, cursing him as a "weak motherfucker." Barry Parker whispered to me that the others were breaking down, and would probably surrender. I hoped he was right, but for the time being, at least, the leader continued to hold sway over the other four, and I was not particularly confident that he could be cajoled into surrendering. The vein in his temple was throbbing, reminding me of how nervous and afraid I myself was. Cautiously raising my arm and pointing a finger directly at him, I slowly, but very plainly, delivered an ultimatum. He tried to interrupt me with more obscenities, but I yelled for him to shut up, which, surprisingly, he did. "Let the officers go and let them go now, or I'll blow your damned head all over the wall," I said as coldly and matter-of-factly as I could.

Please, I prayed, let him believe me. I was risking the safety of the officers, the other staff, and, yes, myself. I had made a stand, and if the inmate just a few feet away from me did not yield I was going to be forced to back up my threat. An eternity passed, and still he did not respond. Then one of the other convicts uttered an obviously frightened "This is crazy!" before the ringleader could again scream for him to shut up. If the others would just surrender, I calculated, maybe he would cave in as well, but he was still successfully intimidating the other hostage takers. Then, in a hideous half-laugh, he asserted scornfully that he would not be easily bullied. "Kill me, I don't give a shit, 'cause when you do, you'll off the pig here too," he hissed through yellowed teeth. An unfamiliar voice was hollering to let another officer through—"He's got the superintendent a shotgun." Jesus, I thought, as I continued to stare at the inmate, he really is going to see this all the way to the end. He had made a believer out of me; he would not be bluffed. For a second, I wondered, What the hell do I do now? There was no backing down. Nevertheless, I almost surprised myself when I blurted out, "Then get ready to die, you bastard." Motioning with my head to the hostage officer who was standing bewildered at knife point, I continued, almost nonchalantly, "He understands that's a risk that goes with the territory. Better he should die with us trying to save him than for me to stand here and let some asshole like you slice his head off. And when I finish with you, I'm just going to go ahead and get those other sons of bitches too."

The officer looked horrified by the whole exchange; I just hoped I had made believers out of the inmates. Holding my hand out, I hollered again for the shotgun. Somebody racked a round in the chamber, making a noise that seemed to bounce off the concrete walls, echoing over and over in my ears. Col. Robert Armstrong then shouted, "Hand this gun to the superintendent!"

Chills traveled up and down my spine. I had challenged the boys, and neither he nor the others were backing off. The ringleader had called my bluff, I agonized. Or had he? Suddenly, the sound of steel could be heard as the shanks hit the floor—the other four inmates had thrown their weapons down and pushed their hostages away. "Don't move," I shouted to them, my eyes still locked on the one holdout. "Get your hands on your heads, and stand back against the wall."

For another second or two, the young convict who stood just a few feet away hung in there. One of the other inmates told him to give it up, but he said nothing. Surveying the circumstances, the boy could see it was all over; still, he made no move. Colonel Armstrong, standing to the right of me, exclaimed, "This punk really thinks he's bad." Abruptly turning to my left, I grabbed for the shotgun behind me. "Damn you!" As I swung back around I almost whooped with joy when the inmate dropped his knife and shoved the officer toward me. It was all over. As I exhaled for what seemed the first time in ten minutes, someone patted my back and uttered a shout of relief. Turning to Colonel Armstrong, I directed him and the other officers to secure the weapons and place the inmates in the segregation unit. There was still much to do. The entire unit had to be searched for weapons and drugs. The inmate hostage takers, as well as other known troublemakers in the unit, needed to be moved immediately. But the worst was over, or so I thought.

As I turned to walk to the sergeant's office, all hell broke loose. The officers moved in to take the inmates into custody, and one of the prisoners at first resisted, then took a swing at Colonel Armstrong. Things quickly degenerated into a brawl, and somehow I ended up on the floor, under a pile of officers and inmates. Thankfully, the inmates had not gotten their hands on their homemade knives again, and the melee was swiftly brought under control.

In spite of such occurrences, Parchman was a relatively quiet prison. Invariably, however, there were constant reminders that never let me forget the nature of the business I was in. The most stark of those were found on death row. Life in Parchman's other camps was no picnic, but "Little Alcatraz" was the worst. In some ways, it was better than a lot of the general population units—it was quiet, only one inmate was confined to a cell, the place was cleaner, and there was not the level of conflict among inmates, or between inmates and officers, that existed in other camps. The negative factors, however, far outweighed any slight advantage to being housed on the row. For nearly five years, I watched in amazement, wondering how men survived the rigors of being confined to a cell for twenty-three hours a day. I would always think of death row first whenever critics assailed the penitentiary as a "country club." Perhaps that is why I made it a point to visit the row as often as time permitted. A "prison within a prison" is a forlorn place, avoided as much as possible by wise inmates. Nor are all prison employees suited to working a unit like "Little Alcatraz." It is a place that exacts a toll in human destruction, in both the keepers and the kept. I was proud of the officers and other staff who worked the death row unit; they did their jobs well, and they treated the condemned men with respect.

Over the course of my first three years as superintendent, I had become somewhat enamored of "Little Alcatraz"—and I had come to know Connie Ray Evans. I never claimed, or presumed, to know him well. I am not certain that anyone who runs a maximum security prison can ever quite be sure that he or she really knows an inmate. For whatever reason, though, I had taken a liking to Connie. He was a pretty ordinary guy who happened to have committed a senseless crime. We did not have much in common, at least not in the beginning. He grew up an impoverished African American youngster in Jackson, Mississippi. Born in Lowell, an economically depressed old textile city north of Boston, I grew up in the quiet little town of Easton. I never attended school with any blacks until I enrolled in Northeastern University. (There was not a single African American family in my hometown.) So Connie and I had nothing in common racially, culturally, or socioeconomically. My family certainly was not wealthy by any means; we were a typically large working-class bunch. Although material wealth was not within our grasp, loving parents and a strict Catholic upbringing more than made up for any financial shortcomings. Working class though we might have been, however, I had no com-

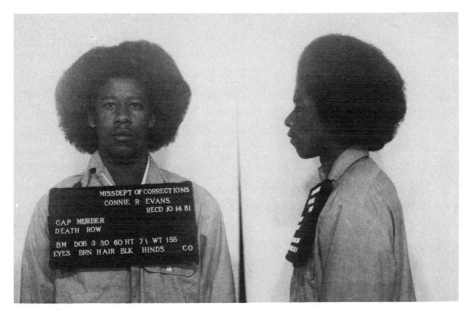

Connie Ray Evans at the time of his admission to Parchman's death row. Evans, who was twenty-seven years old when he was executed, spent five years, eight months, and twenty-three days awaiting his fate.

mon heritage with a young black man who was born in Mississippi amid the turbulence of the civil rights movement. Why or how Connie Ray Evans and I ever developed any kind of relationship will remain a mystery. We had but one thing in common, one thing that bonded us: an octagonal gas chamber that was hidden behind the towers and fences surrounding Parchman's death row unit.

By the time I entered my third full year as superintendent of the Mississippi State Penitentiary, I had come to look forward to my conversations with Connie, even though scheduling did not always permit protracted engagements. He was pleasant to talk to, and he was well liked by the other inmates and by the officers. Oddly, I never gave much thought to the possibility of putting him to death, not until the truth was finally upon us. As I prowled the corridors and cellblocks in the row, I would see the faces of many men who I guessed were destined for that final walk, but Connie Ray Evans was not one of them. Anyhow, there were other problems and situations to be reckoned with. At the time, I had no way of knowing, as the start of a new year approached, that 1987 would be filled with so much sadness.

My boss and close friend, Morris Thigpen, had grown weary of fighting recurring political battles with a few firmly entrenched obstructionist legislators. Having worn the mantle of commissioner of corrections for more than six years, in December 1986 Thigpen announced his departure for a similar position in Alabama. I was appointed to replace Morris as interim corrections commissioner. While I had no burning interest in the job, I was just curious enough to do it until a permanent replacement could be found. Since I needed to relocate temporarily to the department's headquarters in Jackson, I appointed my trusted advisor and closest friend, Wayne Fleming, to take over for me as interim superintendent at Parchman. Had I been able to, I would have taken Wayne to the commissioner's office with me, but I needed him more at the penitentiary. He was a perfect choice to shepherd the place, someone who got along well with the staff and had the respect of the inmates as well. It was an appointment Wayne did not want, and I had a very difficult time convincing him to accept it.

At first uncomfortable and uncertain, Wayne went on to become a more-than-capable administrator. There was never any doubt in my mind that he should be Parchman's next superintendent. Only one problem had plagued Wayne—his health. He had experienced some heart problems, and the doctors diagnosed a very large blood clot in one of his legs, but he eventually returned to work and tackled his duties with renewed determination.

Soon after assuming the superintendent's duties, he fell ill again and entered the hospital in Jackson. Since this facility was just a five-minute drive from my office, I could check on him daily. My family was still living at Parchman, so my evenings were pretty much free to spend with Wayne and his wife, Betty. Then the news came, striking unexpectedly like a great, huge weight: my friend had less than six months to live. Doctors had found a tumor in one of his lungs, and an other one in his brain. At first none of it really sank in, and I argued with Wayne that he should undergo surgery, chemotherapy, or whatever alternatives were available. Wayne and Betty had discussed their options and decided against doing any of those things. He was not so much concerned with prolonging his life as he was with the quality of whatever time he had left. For a while, I was angry that Wayne would not at least try something else. Although respecting the decision he and Betty had arrived at, I understood, but did not want to accept, the fact that he was dying. My best friend was leaving, and there was nothing I could do about it.

Over the last months of his life, Wayne was still my closest confidant, except for my own wife. As each day passed it became more difficult to watch the life ebb from him. So many times, I found myself caught in the most selfish of private battles. I did not want to let go, for he was my best friend, and I knew I would never have another like him. I was going to miss working with him, but I could hardly tolerate watching him suffer what cancer inflicts upon its victims. Through it all, though, he remained more concerned about his family and friends than about himself.

One night I arrived at the hospital to find Wayne more awake and alert than he had been in days. Noting that I seemed more than a little puzzled, Betty shrugged her shoulders and laughingly said that he had talked her head off all day. Wayne wanted to discuss our jobs that evening. Coincidentally, I had been in a meeting that very day with the attorney general and his staff. Edward Earl Johnson was to be executed in less than a month. Though a reprieve was always a distinct possibility, the attorney general was of the opinion that Johnson had run out of time. Wayne and I had discussed executions on other occasions. He had always taken the position that he would prefer not to be involved, though he would do what I asked him to do. Sitting at his bedside, looking at the shadow of a man that lay before me, I wished so much that we could be sidekicks at work again. If ever I needed my friend, I knew it would be in the coming weeks.

Confiding my desire to somehow avoid the execution, I discussed with Wayne all the different emotions and feelings connected with the thing. Insisting that I tried never to forget the victims and their families, I wanted to find a way to rationalize it all. Sometimes, as I wandered about the prison, I would look at the thousands of inmates and think about the incalculable pain they had inflicted on innocent people. It was not always easy, or even possible, to show concern or compassion. Known by the prisoners as a stern disciplinarian, I was a demanding warden to do time under. During my career, I had become convinced that serving a sentence should be unpleasant, the kind of thing that would make a person hate it so much he would never want to do it again. But despite what others might have thought, I had compassion for the inmates, too. Doing time did not mean that a man had to lose his dignity. Nor did it mean that inmates became the property of the state, with no hope of ever paying off their debt to society.

Wayne chided me as I spoke vaguely of being prepared to execute Edward Johnson. Just moments earlier, I had protested having to do it at all. Yes, I had been accused on more than one occasion of having ice-water in my veins, but Wayne knew better. He reminded me of a troubling suicide just a few months earlier.

Suicide is always tragic, but this one was particularly bad, bearing all the trappings of prison life at its worst. The victim was only twenty when he was sentenced to a life term for murder. Married to his high school sweetheart, things had gone sour after a couple of years. He discovered that his wife had been having an affair, and, in a fit of jealousy, he murdered her lover. When the inmate first arrived at

Parchman, he was treated for depression and kept on suicide watch. Eventually transferred to Unit Twenty-Four, a maximum security facility that housed prisoners who were assaultive or otherwise unmanageable in general population units, the inmate chose to end his life there. The boy was a loner who did not associate much with other inmates, and he very seldom gave the officers any trouble. He had been locked down, however, for threatening to stab another inmate.

I was in my morning meeting with Wayne and the associate superintendents when I was notified of the incident. When Wayne and I arrived at the Unit, its administrator, Col. Roger Vanlandingham was already on the scene. His face betrayed what awaited us inside; it was the worst suicide, he said, that he had ever seen. The inmate's cell was up on the second tier, and as Wayne and I climbed the stairs the sound of loud singing drifted from the cellblocks. It was coming from the cell next to the dead inmate's. Politely telling the crooning prisoner to shut up as I hurriedly walked past, I turned and stepped into the bloody room next door. I was shocked by what confronted me. As Wayne entered right behind me, he gasped loudly.

The man's cell was unusually neat, his few possessions arranged meticulously. The inmate had hung himself with one of his shoestrings, tied to a clotheshook on the wall. Although suicidal prisoners commonly choose to hang themselves, looking around the cell I could only shake my head in disbelief. This boy was intent on dying, I thought; no mere cry for help in this case. After hanging himself from the hook, he had removed the blade from a disposable razor and slashed his wrists. Blood had splattered in every direction, covering his face and forming two pools at his feet. This kid wanted to leave nothing to chance. The slash marks were extremely deep, a good inch; what's more, they ran parallel to the arm, rather than across the wrists. A photograph of his wife and baby was found in his shirt pocket.

After two decades in the corrections business, there was very little that could shock me anymore. Suicides were nothing new to me— they are unfortunate realities of the prison world. Although I had never got used to the violence or the abject hopelessness and despair, this particular suicide stunned me as the most brutal I had ever seen. I found it impossible to keep my eyes off the boy's face—even in death, he seemed pained. Wayne stepped back into the cell and handed me an envelope. Inside was a suicide note and a copy of the divorce papers that he had received from his wife. In his personal correspondence we found letters between the two of them that detailed the intense pain and degradation he had felt. The contents of his suicide note would have caused the coldest of hearts to break. Quietly I told the officers to cut him down. One of them reminded me that the coroner had not yet arrived and that the body should not be moved. "Christ, let him have just a shred of dignity," I barked. "Cut him down!"

In many ways, I was always more frustrated by prison suicides than by almost any other kind of death in the joint. I looked at the young prisoner as he was taken down from the wall, his neck bruised and swollen from the shoestring tightly wound around it. How much pain he must have been in, how alone and hopeless he must have felt to have taken his own life. Trying to imagine the depth of his despair, I wondered if there was anything we could have done to prevent his suicide. What can you do to encourage a twenty-year-old kid who has a life sentence to look forward to? My eyes filled with tears as I thought about my own family, and how I would feel if I ever lost them.

As I stepped back out on the tier, the inmate next door asked to speak to me. He knew his neighbor had planned to commit suicide, he said. In fact, he boasted, he could just about pinpoint the time he did it. Somewhat naïvely, I asked the prisoner if he had made any attempt to dissuade him or had tried to alert an officer. "Not my problem," he placidly replied. "Convict wants to check out, it ain't my concern." I was furious, not so much at the inmate as at a system that engendered and fostered such callous disregard for life. Maybe it should not have bothered me; I knew a lot of people who would just shrug and say it was one less convict to worry about. But I could not forget what John Collier had told me so long ago—we are supposed to be better than that. Life was cheap enough in the joint. But I had five thousand inmates, and one lousy psychiatrist, one clinical psychologist. How were we supposed to help anyone when the odds were like that? It was another needless, senseless death.

Nearing the end of his life, Wayne was feeling tired, his weak voice slowly drifting off, as he reminded me that I could not avoid the execution of Edward Earl Johnson. I interrupted, assuring him that I knew it was my duty to carry it out. Then Wayne opened his eyes, smiled, and said that was not what he meant—it was my duty to be there for the inmate. "Whatever else the Johnson boy may be," my friend whispered, "he's a human being, and he's entitled to some compassion too. If not you, then who will give a damn? Who will care?" I had protested earlier that I was ready, should I be required to supervise an execution; yet, as I left the hospital that night, I recalled Wayne Fleming's gentle, cautionary question: "How in the world," he asked in true bewilderment, "do you get ready for something like that?"

As the first weeks of May approached, I asked myself that over and over. With each passing day, the answer became more painfully obvious. There was nothing I could do to truly prepare myself. I talked to my wife about it, discussed it with my parish priest, even spoke with the bishop of my diocese. Try as I might, there were no easy answers, no way for me to know what to expect. Late at night I would find myself pondering one question above all—why me? How was it that I was intended to have a role in putting another human being to death? There were but a handful of men who had supervised executions since the Gary Gilmore debacle in 1977. Out of the hundreds of millions of people in the United States, I was about to become one of a dozen or so who could lay claim to the dubious distinction of having lawfully killed another human being.

As the execution date loomed nearer, I felt the pressure increase every day. I tried diligently to carry on with other normal business, for the penitentiary had to continue to operate. Johnson's final days passed quickly. The deputy wardens were pretty much saddled with keeping the prison running, while I spent most of my waking hours dealing with execution preparations, and my dying friend. Frustrated at being surrounded by death, and powerless to do anything about it, I would sometimes feel nothing but disgust as I entered Wayne's hospital room. Symbolically, there was little difference between his room and Edward Johnson's death row cell. Repeatedly, I found myself making the most asinine comparisons. What did Johnson want for a last meal? What, if anything, did Wayne eat today? How is Edward Johnson doing today? How is Wayne feeling today? Any signs of erratic behavior? What is his mood like?

And then there was my other friend, Connie Ray Evans. He and Earl, as he referred to Johnson, had become friends. They had arrived on the row within a short time of each other. Connie believed in Johnson's innocence and spoke of it frequently. Did I think Johnson had killed a man, Connie asked me one afternoon shortly before the execution. I tried to avoid the question, choosing the easy way out. The courts had found him guilty and had reviewed his appeals numerous times, I repeated matter-of-factly. It was not up to prison officials to debate a convict's innocence or guilt. Connie pressed on, however. What if I, as a prison official, was convinced Johnson was innocent— knew he was innocent? What would I do? I protested that I would have no way of knowing that. I did not investigate the crime, prosecute the case, or sit as a juror. "Damn it, Mr. C., just answer the question straight and honest. If you had evidence in your hands that Earl was innocent, what would you do?" Connie was uncharacteristically agitated, frustrated with what he perceived as my attempts to avoid answering truthfully. Finally, I said I would probably present the matter to the governor; the final decision would be up to him. Connie sprang to his feet, rattling his cell door in anger, and bitterly asserted, "Yeah, it's good to have someone else to blame. Y'all always accuse us of blaming our parents, schoolteachers—anybody but ourselves for ending up in the joint. Hell, Warden, y'all do it too. You didn't commit the crime, Earl did. You didn't convict him, the jury did. You didn't sentence him to die—the judge or the jury or some damn body else did. And when you kill him, it ain't really you that's doin' that, either. It's the state, the folks out there that's doin' it."

I thought for a moment that maybe I was supposed to say something, reply in some way that would make him understand. What the hell would it be, I wondered. What could I possibly say that would make sense? I left the cell without saying a word. Connie's outburst was unusual, but he was entitled to it. Hell, they all were. Watching preparations for an execution must be almost as tough on those waiting in line as it is on the one being executed. That is all it is, one long line, in which each man has to wait his turn—watching others ahead of him go one at a time.

While the Johnson execution was filled with media hype, he was rather unremarkable as condemned prisoners go. He lacked, for example, the notoriety of Jimmy Lee Gray, the last man to have been put to death in Mississippi's gas chamber, four years earlier. Gray, a man everyone loved to hate, had brutally raped and murdered a three-year-old girl in Pascagoula, after having been paroled from the Arizona correctional system for another brutal crime.

Edward Earl Johnson was not a despised child killer, though his crime was no less despicable. Convicted of shooting a town marshal in cold blood, he initially confessed, but later recanted, claiming the confession was coerced. He would maintain his innocence until his dying breath. His execution drew a lot of media attention, with reporters traveling from as far away as New York to cover the event. Also present was a film crew from the British Broadcasting Corporation. About a year earlier, the BBC had been granted permission by the Mississippi Board of Corrections to make a documentary at Parchman concerning the death penalty. The focus of the film was to be on the effect of carrying out an execution on the staff and inmates of the penitentiary. Edward Johnson had agreed to permit the crew to film the final two weeks leading up to his execution. *Fourteen Days in May* was shown first overseas, before being presented in the United States on the cable channel Home Box Office. It was a landmark documentary—the most revealing "inside" glimpse of the execution protocol that had ever been filmed in the United States. Although the BBC crew was extremely professional, and as unobtrusive as possible, their presence simply added to the pressure that bore down on the prison because of all the media attention.

I had determined very early in the planning process for the execution of Edward Earl Johnson that disruptions of normal penitentiary operations would be minimized as much as possible. From conversations with prison staff, legislators, and media representatives, I fully understood that the Jimmy Lee Gray execution had become a bureaucratic nightmare. In all fairness to the corrections administrators, Gray's execution had been Mississippi's first in twenty years, so it was reasonable to engage in some rather detailed planning. Where to locate anti–death penalty demonstrators, what to do with pro–death penalty activists, how to handle the crush of media people—all were legitimate problems that any prison had to be prepared for during an execution. It was my judgment, however, based on information I received and documents I reviewed, that the institution had all but become a heavily armed fortress. Employees, as well as other officials, found themselves being stopped at a dozen different security checkpoints. The penitentiary was placed on lockdown a full seventy-two hours before the execution, increasing the tension among prisoners and adding to the aura of media hype that normally surrounds such events.

I wanted to avoid as much of that as possible. Other than the normal processing of visitors at the front gate, only one additional security checkpoint was established for the Johnson execution—at the entrance to the death row unit itself. We also greatly simplified the identification process. A green clip-on card was issued to all execution team members, and a yellow clip-on card was given to official witnesses. If people did not possess such identification, they were not permitted access to death row.

I did not order the prison placed on lockdown status until four o'clock in the afternoon, only eight hours before the execution; unless we encountered some unexpected difficulties, the lockdown order would be lifted as soon as possible after Edward Earl Johnson had been put to death.

The most significant change that I made in execution procedures, and the one for which I was most severely criticized by certain elements of the staff, concerned Johnson's final visitors. I had issued instructions to permit his immediate family to have contact visits with him during the two weekends preceding the execution. I also allowed them to visit on Monday and Tuesday, terminating the final visit at nine-thirty on the evening he was to be executed. Some of the deputy wardens and ranking security staff expressed grave reservations about such liberal visitation hours. By allowing the family to remain with him until just two or three hours before the execution, we ran the risk of an emotional scene at the end of the visiting time. Many encouraged me to cut off visitation the Sunday before the execution. What concerned my critics most, however, was the physical contact. Death row prisoners normally are allowed to visit only in noncontact situations, separated by a screen or a plate of shatterproof glass. In the end, I decided to take a chance by allowing Johnson to have contact visits with his family.

As it turned out, the visits never caused so much as a ripple. The inmate and his family behaved appropriately and were extremely cooperative. There were no outbursts or agitated behavior when the last visit was terminated. Some quiet sobs, silent hugs, and sad farewells were all that passed between Edward Earl Johnson and his loved ones.

I was probably more on edge about impending events than my condemned prisoner was. At least on the surface, he appeared to be remarkably calm and at peace with himself. During those last few days he spent considerable time with his family, lawyers, and personal minister, as well as with Ron Padgett, the chaplain at Parchman. I found myself making a conscious effort to have as little contact with him as possible, thinking it would make it easier for me to carry out my duties. I could not completely avoid him, of course, and one of our stranger meetings occurred the Sunday evening before the execution. I was with him alone in his cell for a brief time, probably no more than twenty minutes. I asked if he had any special requests for a last meal. What a really curious thing to have to inquire about, I thought. How cold it must have sounded; it felt terribly impersonal just to be asking. "Yes," he said softly, "fried shrimp." After we settled that bit of business, I asked if his family would be returning to visit him on Monday and Tuesday. His response was a curious blend of gratitude and regret. After thanking me for allowing him to have contact visits with his family, he stared at the bare floor of his cell for a minute. "I want them here, and yet I don't," he responded dejectedly.

Silently nodding that I understood what he meant, I began to explain quietly that we would shortly be moving him to the last cell on the tier, the one closest to the death house, the last-night cell. An officer would be posted outside his cell, around the clock, until it was time to go. Edward sighed and shrugged his shoulders. Then looking at me, not with hate or contempt, but with resignation, he smiled slightly and said he would not think of "screwing" the state out of its chance to kill him. Finally, I was obliged to ask if he would like to receive some kind of tranquilizer just prior to the execution. It was then that Edward's words betrayed the bitterness that hid just beneath the surface. "No," he replied sardonically, "I want a clear mind when you walk me in there. Will you be needing one for yourself?" Getting up from his bunk, where I had been sitting, I gave a somewhat tentative "no." Oh, I knew I would not be taking anything, though I presumed that I would probably feel like it. Standing at the cell door, with his back to me, Edward Earl Johnson exclaimed, "Good, 'cause I want you to have a clear mind too. I want you to know exactly what you're doing when you execute me. I want you to remember every last detail, 'cause I'm innocent, Mr. Cabana . . . I'm innocent."

He had maintained his innocence for nearly seven years, and why not? He had appeals pending all that time. One could hardly expect a condemned man to try and escape the death house without proclaiming his innocence. But what about Connie Ray Evans, I wondered. He admitted his guilt, knowing full well the crime carried the death penalty. Somehow, I did not believe Johnson was innocent. I had been through his case file a dozen times. I was very familiar with the allegedly coerced confession, and the questionable identification by a woman whom Johnson had supposedly attempted to assault before shooting the town marshal. None of what he claimed seemed to be true. Anyhow, his case had been reviewed by federal courts numerous times. Surely, if there were even the slightest hint that he had not committed the crime, the federal district court or the U.S. Fifth Circuit Court of Appeals would have intervened long ago. Hastily leaving his cell, I motioned for the staff to begin moving him. Johnson called to the inmate in the cell next to him, asking if he wanted his radio when he was gone. There was no reply.

After my conversation with Edward Johnson that Sunday evening, I was not really looking forward to the next couple of hours. The gas chamber had been thoroughly inspected in recent days and appeared to be in working order, but a live test was necessary; I scheduled two trials for late Sunday evening. First, we would run through the procedures exactly as they were to be carried out on Wednesday morning. The idea was for the execution team to go through the protocol to make certain there were no mechanical problems or human errors. I found a volunteer on the staff who approximated Johnson in physique and size. I had an absolute dread that something might go wrong. Standing outside the rear entrance to the execution room, I smoked one cigarette after another while preparations for the test were under way. Officers inside slammed the metal windows along Edward Johnson's cellblock tightly shut, and I wondered what must be going through his mind, knowing we were getting ready to test the chamber.

When everyone was assembled, the chaplain and I escorted our make-believe prisoner, Shep Haga, into the chamber. The heat was unbearable, even though it was nine o'clock in the evening. Large beads of sweat covered Shep's forehead as we took him in from the last-night cell. Quickly, the officers strapped him in the chair and secured his head with the restraint device that had been added since the last, controversial execution in 1983. I stared at the infamous metal pole that stood directly behind the chair, the one against which Jimmy Lee Gray had repeatedly struck his head, curious as to why anyone would have intentionally placed it there. Hell, I thought, in 1954, when the gas chamber was installed at Parchman, no one was too concerned about executions being aesthetically pleasing.

All around me team members were discussing procedures and instructions. Dr. Bennie Wright briefly stepped into the chamber, attaching two long stethoscopes and the leads for the EKG monitor to Shep's chest. In a bit of gallows humor, I stepped in to simulate the reading of the death warrant; looking at Shep, I chuckled and said, "Say your good-byes, boy." Then the chamber was quickly sealed as we began to go through a lengthy checklist of procedures. Standing at the observation window, next to Doctor Wright, I was amazed by the reading on the EKG monitor. The staff volunteer's heart rate was wildly erratic, and the doctor wondered aloud what Johnson's would be like Wednesday morning.

Shep was becoming increasingly uncomfortable in the chamber (a condition clearly documented by the EKG monitor). When I ordered the chamber unsealed, there was one last bit of death house humor—Shep Haga yelled, "Get me out of here, these mosquitoes are wearing me out!" Everyone enjoyed a hearty laugh, and though such humor would seem inappropriate to the casual observer, it struck me at the time as a necessary respite from the pall that hung over us.

Soon enough, however, we all realized there would be no more jokes or laughter, not for a while, anyway. After getting Shep out of the chamber, we brought in two rabbits in a small cage; they were to be our live subjects for the actual operational test. It was all so simple, and it went quite smoothly. The chamber worked with chilling efficiency. They were only rabbits, yet the silence in the execution room was deafening. As I looked around me, everyone was quiet, eyes glued to the chamber. We were all surprised at how small the cloud of gas looked as it slowly drifted upward. The rabbits began to sniff the air anxiously, frantically moving about the cages. They quickly started flopping about violently, and in a matter of seconds it was over. I tried to assure myself that if all went as neatly on Wednesday morning it would not be so bad. Admittedly, I had been stunned by the brutality of the test. Still, I knew my opinions would sound silly to anyone else, so I stayed quiet. They were only rabbits, after all, but it was just a little more ugly and violent than I had counted on.

Maybe the real thing would not be quite so bad. The inmate would be strapped securely into the chair; he would not flop around. One or two deep breaths and it would all be over. Dwight Presley, whom I had appointed acting superintendent in Wayne Fleming's absence, slipped into the darkness with me. He, too, silent at first, lit up a cigarette. Then, exhaling long and slowly, he gripped my arm and whispered hoarsely, "Jesus Christ, can you imagine what the hell that thing does to a man?"

Staring at the row of windows that ran along the top of Edward Johnson's cellblock, the prisoner's emphatic "I'm innocent" reverberated in my ears. No wonder he said he wanted me to have a clear mind. It was small consolation, but at least I knew I was not totally alone with my feelings of revulsion. Dwight had also been disturbed by what he had just witnessed. He was right—if a couple of rabbits re-acted that violently, how much worse would it be for a man?

"No," I abruptly said to Presley. "I don't want to imagine. Hell, I just want it to be over!"

Midnight Sunrise

Life after death? What do you tell a man
who has only twelve hours to live?

Clinton T. Duffy, Warden, San Quentin Prison

Marvin Wiggins was the most notable figure ever to occupy the warden's chair at the Mississippi State Penitentiary. He served longer than any other man in that capacity, from 1944 until his retirement in 1956. During this "golden age," Parchman was the envy of politicians and correctional practitioners alike. Sadly, as so often happens in corrections, following a brilliant administrative career Wiggins left the penitentiary somewhat broken and embittered.

During his tenure, Wiggins managed to gather considerable political clout, especially in the halls of the state capitol in Jackson. He was not shy about calling in political favors whenever he deemed it necessary. By the early 1950s, however, his political influence and popularity were beginning to diminish, and in 1954 he would lose the biggest battle of his political life. In the 1930s, on humanitarian grounds, Mississippi had chosen to substitute electrocution for hanging as its preferred method of execution. Unlike many states, however, Mississippi continued to carry out executions in the county where the crime had occurred. This had posed no problem so long as hanging was involved; a gallows could be constructed quite easily almost anywhere. Electrocution was another matter, however. Certainly, neither the state nor the counties could afford to install an electric chair in each county jail or courthouse. Characteristically, the Mississippi legislature decided to use a portable electric chair, which could be transported from county to county as necessary. This rather ingenious method of dispatching the state's worst felons prevailed for the next two decades.

Then, ever mindful of technological advancements, the legislature decided to change Mississippi's method of execution once again. The portable electric chair had certainly been effective, but the legislators eventually decided that the gas chamber was more in keeping with civilized standards of putting convicts to death. As before, however, they faced the problem of how to do it. Gas chambers simply could not be carted around on the back of a truck from courthouse to courthouse. It was also not feasible economically to construct a gas chamber in each county. The only viable option was to build one at Parchman. A tremendous political struggle ensued. Marvin Wiggins was fiercely opposed to locating the gas chamber in "his" penitentiary; an execution was, in his opinion, a task appropriate for sheriffs and county courthouse crowds, but not for Parchman. The warden called in any political favor ever owed to him. The old warhorse had won many battles before, but this time the opposition was too powerful, and before long he found a gas chamber sitting in the midst of Parchman's cotton fields.

Losing the battle was almost more than he could bear, especially since it was his second major defeat at the hands of a group of legislative young turks. Earlier, also over the warden's vehement objections, the legislature had passed a bill authorizing construction of a maximum security unit at Parchman, something the prison had never used before. Wiggins did not ask for it, nor did he want it. He had seen enough of northern and western prisons, with their tiers upon tiers of cellblocks, twenty-foot walls, and gun towers, to know that was not what he wanted or Parchman needed. The legislature, however, remained adamant and eventually triumphed. Much to his chagrin, Wiggins watched "Little Alcatraz" rise from the dusty Delta ground, anathema to everything he believed about penology.

Once a maximum security unit at the penitentiary was constructed, the issue of where to locate a gas chamber and a death row became moot—there was no place as logical as Parchman. Not long after the gas chamber had been completed it was scheduled to receive its initial occupants. The first man to occupy the black chair was Gerald Gallego, a cold-blooded killer who would be one of the worst convicts ever to go to his death at Parchman. But then, how do you make such comparisons, especially when all victims cry out from their graves for justice? I, for example, doubted that anyone ever executed at Parchman could have been more deserving than Jimmy Lee Gray, a depraved rapist and murderer. The inability of the state to execute him for his crime against three-year-old Dressa Scales had frustrated proponents of the death penalty for ten years. His was a vicious act of wanton brutality, yet even his much-demanded execution raised howls of protest concerning the way in which it was carried out.

For Marvin Wiggins, that first execution was the lowest point of his career. Being required to participate was galling enough, but the events that followed would trouble the old man forever after. Gallego was ushered into the gas chamber and strapped down. Moments later, the warden gave the order to proceed. The lever dropped the deadly load of cyanide crystals, but nothing happened. There was just a wispy cloud of gas, ever so slight, that arose from beneath the chamber. Gallego coughed violently, struggled against the straps that bound him, and continued to breathe. Marvin Wiggins's worst nightmare had come true! The executioner had failed to measure the ingredients correctly, and the inmate was still fully conscious. Nearly half an hour later, after the required corrections were made, the chamber was once again pronounced ready. The scene, however, had taken its toll on the condemned man, the witnesses, and, most of all, on the warden. He was never quite the same after that. The thought of a botched execution, whether due to mechanical failure or human error, is something that no corrections official wants to entertain. The image of a man inhaling enough poisonous gas to make him violently ill, but not enough to prove lethal, is a concept that is totally foreign to most people. Marvin Wiggins lived it.

June 1987 passed rapidly, with the execution of Connie Ray Evans looming just around the corner. I had neither seen nor talked with him in almost two weeks, even though I had received a note from Connie asking to speak to me about his execution. It had been on my desk for several days, unanswered. After my experiences of the previous few weeks, I was tired of dealing with death and violence.

Edward Johnson's execution had barely come and gone when I was notified that Connie was next. There was no recovery time, no opportunity to get back to normal, whatever that was. We simply went from analyzing the operations and procedures in one execution to beginning to prepare for another.

Within a few days of Johnson's execution, I lost my best friend. Wayne had implored Betty and his doctors to let him return home to die, and I was glad he could be surrounded by family and friends at Parchman. I did miss seeing him every day, since I was still working in Jackson and could return home myself only on weekends. Wayne and I had already said our good-byes while he was still in the hospital, on one of the last nights I had an opportunity to spend with him and Betty. We talked of many things, but mostly of living. Though Wayne drifted in and out of sleep, there was nothing wrong with his mind that night; he even managed to elicit a good laugh when he apologized for not hanging around longer—he had "places to go and people to meet." As we sat through the night, snatching bits and pieces of conversation, I was struck by how much at peace he was. The subject of death came up several times, but never in a morose way. For Wayne, death was the next leg of a marvelous journey. If life on this earth is truly meant to serve as a chance for us to make a contribution, to make the world a better place, then Wayne had done his job.

As I sat on the side of the bed holding his hand gently in mine, Wayne thanked me for being his friend. It was I who should be thanking him, I protested. My friend could no longer see very well, and his voice was weak, but on that night he had the vision and the strength to see inside, touching a cauldron of emotions that I had seldom permitted myself to experience. For twenty years I had worked in a profession that left little room for emotions or feelings. Even before that, however, I had learned to mask my feelings (particularly compassion), lest I subject myself to hurtful experiences. In Viet Nam, the sight of mangled bodies burned beyond recognition, shiny metal coffins stacked one atop the other, and the corpses of women and children—all dampened displays of emotion. You became hardened to it, for the sake of your own sanity. The prison environment was not much different from a combat zone—savagery, wasted lives, lost opportunities, no opportunities at all. The penitentiary encourages a mindset that revolves around aloneness. An upside-down world in which everything and everyone is suspect, a simple act of kindness, perhaps nothing more significant than a word of encouragement, is viewed as suspicious by the staff and as weakness by the inmates. Prison, after all, is a macho environment where the emphasis is often placed on batons and guns, Mace and handcuffs.

I had been part of that world so long that I, too, kept a constant vigil for any sign of personal weakness. There were rare instances when I would let my guard down, but I was always embarrassed, almost afraid to show any signs of emotion or compassion. Yet, as Wayne Fleming and I quietly said our good-byes, I no longer feared what anyone else would think. Wayne had a way of getting beneath someone's exterior, aiming right for the heart. Reaching up and rubbing my shoulder, he smiled and said, in the most soothing voice, "I love you, my friend; I love you so much." There were no barriers anymore, no invisible walls that dictated how I could feel or not feel. The tears came, and they ran freely as I told Wayne that I loved him, too. His own face wet, we hugged, without saying a word, for a very long time. As I cradled my friend's head in my arms, I silently prayed for his fight to be over soon. After a while, I laughingly asked him what he thought the staff and inmates would think if they saw the warden crying, and Betty started laughing too. Knowing how most of the officers at Parchman felt about homosexual inmates, she snickered, "They would lose their minds if they saw this! It's not every day that a couple of ugly old prison superintendents hug and cry!" We all let loose a loud burst of laughter; it was a joke that only some old prison warhorses like us could have enjoyed. I bade my friend goodnight, and he whispered to me not to be sad. Wayne was truly a remarkable man, remarkable for who he was. He was genuine and sincere, honest and loyal. Despite the pain of watching him suffer, even his dying taught me much about being alive.

When Wayne Fleming passed away just a few weeks later, I knew I could not replace him, either as colleague or friend. More important,

Parchman would miss him, and that was perhaps the saddest realization of all. The need was great for more people of Wayne's caliber in the corrections field, but such men come along but rarely in this world.

Finally, in response to Connie Ray Evans's note, I made myself go to the death row unit. Trudging down the cellblocks, I spoke dutifully to a few inmates, but I did not stop to talk with any of them. I was there to see Connie, and I was not overly enthusiastic about that. It had nothing to do with not wanting to talk to him—I had just had too much of death and dying.

The door to Evans's cell groaned open, and I assured the hesitant officer that it was okay to leave me alone with the inmate. Connie's attitude was pretty upbeat, considering all the hurdles he faced. Some small talk set the stage for the details that needed discussing. What the hell is the sense in asking a condemned man what he wants to eat for a last meal, I wondered. Why even bother with a special meal? But, dutifully, I asked Connie what he wanted to eat, sensing all the time the anger within him, a jarring reminder of his impending fate. The question brought a rapid response, and an equally sudden change in attitude—"What am I supposed to want? I mean, what difference does it make?" His anger welled up as he passionately argued the futility of it all. "It's like another little piece of the game, another bit of torture. Here, man, here's a steak and baked potato. Enjoy, 'cause in a couple hours we're going to gas you."

Leaning against the cell door, my back to the empty tier, I folded my arms and stared at the floor. Connie paced back and forth in the cramped cell. Reaching up to turn his television off, he pounded the set with his fist. Bowing his head and sighing deeply, he asked about visitation. I told him I would permit him to meet with his immediate family from Friday morning right on up to about nine or nine-thirty the night of the execution. Expressing appreciation for the offer, he stated rather matter-of-factly that he would not see his family after Sunday. I asked if that was what they wanted or if he had made the decision on his own. "It's just better that way, that's all," he replied somewhat testily. "My mama's got a bad heart condition, and my daddy's in bad health too. No, I want it over with Sunday." I understood his reasons, but I suggested that he also think about his family's wishes. "Do not be impulsive," I warned him. "Look," he shot back, "I want you to promise me that if any of my family tries to visit me after Sunday, you'll stop them." With hands in my back pockets, it was my turn to start pacing. "Connie, I don't know if you really want to do that," I muttered. Impatient with my reply, his anger momentarily boiled over. "Damn it, it's my right to refuse to see any visitor, and you know you can't make me. Just do your job, Warden, and don't let them in if they show up after Sunday."

As I moved a couple of steps toward him, my hands shot out of my pockets, coming to rest on my hips and giving me an assertive pose. "Don't tell me my job, you just do yours!" I shouted. "*You* tell your family you don't want to see them after Sunday, because I'm not going to do your dirty work for you!"

I fumbled through my pockets searching for a cigarette and lighter, and, after taking an extra-long drag, I sheepishly offered one to Connie. His face brightened, and then, with a mock frown, he reminded me that "those things will kill you." I wanted out of that cell. It was unbearably hot, even with his small fan blowing, and I was drenched in sweat. But I mainly wanted to go because I felt awkward and unsure of myself— not in control. I was not used to the feeling; I was pretty much accustomed to being in charge and having things my way. Tossing the cigarette into the toilet, I told Connie I had some other things to do, and turned quickly toward the cell door.

"Wait a minute," he blurted, "I want to know about it." I gripped the steel bars with one hand, waving the other in frustration. Without looking at him, I tried to bargain my way out. I pleaded that there was not enough time and promised to return later, but he was determined not to be put off. Bolting across the cell, he stood just inches away from me, grabbing the cell door and shaking it violently. "You've got all the time you want," he screamed, shaking the cell door again for emphasis. An officer sprinted down the tier to investigate the commotion, but I waved him off. "It's all right," I said, "it's all right." The officer, unconvinced, stood looking at me for a moment. "Really!" I said, "I promise!" The officer slowly walked back down the tier, and Connie began speaking again, this time in a subdued tone that suggested an extreme effort on his part to control the anger and frustration he was feeling.

"God damn it," he hissed through clenched teeth, "I'm the one that ain't got time. Damn it, Warden, I have a right to know, I need to know what you're going to do to me in there." His voice was trembling, almost breaking as he spoke.

Taking a deep breath, I stepped back from the door and sat down on his bunk. When I finally allowed my eyes to meet his, he nervously cleared his throat and mumbled an apologetic "Sorry." Before I could say anything, Connie asked if he would experience any pain. Frustrated, I answered halfheartedly that I did not know, but probably not. Then, just as quickly, I apologized; I too was angry and impatient, but not with him. Curiously, I suddenly said, "Breathe." He looked at me, his expression a mixture of puzzlement and fright. "Breathe," I said again, "breathe real deep. You'll know when it's time. Just look at me, I'll be standing in front of the window." For a second or two, I could not believe what I was telling him, but I had grown tired of trying to avoid it. Besides, he was correct, he had a right to know what would happen to him, how it would happen. I continued explaining, my voice trailing off as I did so. "I'll tell you, I'll . . . I guess I'll nod my head or something. Hell, I don't know, Connie; you'll just know, okay?" It was my turn to shake. The palms of my hands were slippery with sweat. I softly cursed the heat as I finished the grim task of telling him what to expect. "When I give you the signal, just start taking slow, deep breaths. You'll be able to hear the lever drop. When it does, just close your eyes and breathe. You'll be unconscious in a matter of seconds." He said nothing, but slowly began pacing again. Somehow, his lean, muscular frame seemed to stoop. I got up and stepped to the door again, determined to leave. Edward Earl Johnson had not asked anything about the procedure; he did not want to know. I thought to myself how much better I liked it that way.

Without another word, Connie crawled onto his bunk and curled up into a fetal position. Hollering for an officer to let me out, I turned to speak, but fell silent as I watched the condemned man pull a pencil from beneath his mattress. Reaching up to a calendar on the wall, he marked an X across the square that read July 1. He had circled July 7, his execution date. The loud grinding noise of the heavy steel door sliding open broke the silence that had descended on the cell. I hastily departed, leaving Connie Ray Evans alone with his thoughts. Sobs only partially muffled by the pillow covering his face, followed me as I left the death row unit.

It was already well past dinnertime, and at eight o'clock we would test the chamber on some rabbits. "Of course the thing works," I had been assured by staff. It had operated flawlessly just a few weeks before for the Johnson execution. I was not taking any chances, however, for even if the chamber was mechanically sound our procedures required some improvements. I had escorted Johnson into the chamber about five minutes before midnight, presuming the chemicals would be ready. As soon as I received a call from the attorney general giving final clearance, I gave the order to proceed. The chemicals, though, were not quite prepared, requiring about five more minutes before they were ready for use. Every second seemed like an hour. Johnson asked several times what I was waiting for, finally shouting, "Let's go! Let's go!" After a couple more minutes passed, he started singing a gospel hymn. Finally, the chemicals were pronounced ready, and Edward Earl Johnson was put to death. The delay had been agonizingly long, and I was determined such a situation would not happen again. The test run would allow us to straighten out any procedural problems.

The checklist for the gas chamber has some two dozen steps; before running the test on the rabbits later in the evening, we went through all the steps several times to ensure that everyone was absolutely certain of his responsibilities. Finally, Steve Puckett carried the caged rabbits into the chamber, placing them in the chair. Roger Vanlandingham was the officer responsible for pouring the cyanide crystals into the receptacle under the chair. I was standing in the doorway as he took the cap off the jar and crouched down to start the cyanide on its way. Strangely, the crystals disappeared from view, and it took a few seconds before anyone realized that something was amiss. Then, Roger bolted upright and yelled to get out of the chamber. The crystals were going down the small shaft directly into the sulfuric acid, producing a small, willowy-looking, deadly cloud. After repeatedly running through the checklist, none of us had noticed the lever in the down position. Consequently, the dish that holds the cyanide was already sitting in the acid, and the seven of us who were in the room at the time could have been killed. The experience shook all of us, and it convinced me of the need to ask the legislature to immediately eliminate the gas chamber as the method of execution in Mississippi. After settling our nerves, we carried out the test without any more complications. As expected, the chamber worked flawlessly.

The next day I met with Connie Evans again, although somewhat hurriedly. Choosing not to see him in his cell, I had him escorted to the sergeant's office, where I instructed the officers to remove him from the restraint gear. The sergeant poked his head in the door and asked if he could speak with me for a moment. He told me that Connie had not slept much during the night and was pretty agitated. "Great," I responded sarcastically: I was there to talk to him about what arrangements he and his family wished to make for disposal of his body, which ought to put him in an even better frame of mind. The wiry middle-aged sergeant stood impassively, maneuvering a huge wad of chewing tobacco around his cheek. Pushing his baseball-style cap back, revealing a rapidly receding hairline, he shrugged and asked if I would let them leave the restraint gear on the inmate. I understood his caution, but I did not believe Connie posed much of a threat. The sergeant nodded and said that, just to be on the safe side, he would wait right outside the door.

I walked around the desk and flopped down in the wobbly old swivel chair. Asking Connie how he was doing, I pointed at the cushioned chair sitting by the desk and motioned for him to sit down. Without hesitation, standing, with a defiant look in his eyes, he forcefully let me know how he was doing. "Did you test that thing last night?" he asked scornfully. I quickly responded that we had. "Jesus Christ," he thundered, "you actually tested the damned thing?" His face registered bewilderment and disbelief. The sergeant and another officer looked in on us, but I held my hand up and shook my head. Still refusing to sit down, Connie took a couple of steps to his right and leaned against the wall. "You're so fucking sure you'll get to kill me. I can't believe it, I mean, hell, I've still got a few days left. My lawyers are still working."

"Knock it off, Connie, enough of the bullshit," I growled. "You think I want to do this, that I'm looking forward to it? If you do, if you truly believe that, then you don't really know me." Casting a pained glance at me, he shook his head and spoke with a bitterness I had not heard before. "I thought you were my friend. Well, maybe not a friend, but . . . hell, I don't know what I mean. Isn't the execution enough? Is all this other crap really necessary?"

Searching for answers that might make some sense to him, I folded my hands and finally explained that the test was necessary for humanitarian reasons. His face bore a deep frown, lips drawn tightly into a pencil-thin line, but he said nothing. I quickly related the story of Gerald Gallego's execution many years before. Even though it was a gruesome way to make a point, I wanted him to understand the necessity of testing the chamber. I tried to speak carefully, aware that he was already extremely nervous and upset. As I finished laying out the unnerving facts of the Gallego execution, Connie began to speak very slowly, mumbling all but incoherently, his moist eyes staring at the floor. "Do I have to wear this?" he asked, referring to the red jumpsuit that all death row prisoners were required to wear. I shook my head no. "You can wear regular inmate clothing if you'd like—blue pants and a blue shirt," I responded.

Judging by the expression on his face he wanted to say something more, but was struggling. I tried coaxing him, but made a hasty retreat when I saw his eyes welling with tears. He fought to beat them back while I sat there silently thinking how glad I was that he was capable of demonstrating emotion. I felt for him and wanted to console him, but I did not know how. There was nothing I could say or do that would change things. The reality of it all was staring at both of us. So many tears. A man was dead, and surely his widow and children had shed countless tears. I felt sad for them, too. And then there were Connie's parents. How many nights had they cried? There was enough pain to last both families a lifetime.

"Mr. Cabana," he stammered, the anger suddenly absent from his voice, "Some of the other guys . . . well, they said . . . I mean . . . will I mess on myself? I don't want to be embarrassed or anything." It struck me like a sledgehammer in the pit of my stomach. How pitiable the human condition that it should all come down to a question like that. Patiently, I told him it was not something to worry about. He responded pensively that he guessed that it did not really matter anyway. As I got up and walked around the desk, I told him I would be seeing him on Sunday, adding "I wish you'd reconsider letting your family see you Monday or Tuesday." He nodded and said he would. "Thanks. I'm sorry," he offered; "I know it's not your fault."

Connie visited with his family all day Saturday and Sunday. True to his word, though, he told them he did not want them to come back Monday or Tuesday. Leaving the sergeant's office on Sunday as Connie shared a final, tearful embrace with his mother, I thought about my own mother, and how painful it would be for me one day to say a last farewell to her. Stepping toward the front entrance, I stood there alone for a very long moment, watching a heartbroken mother cling desperately to her son. As I looked around, I noticed an officer standing by the case manager's office door, along with Chaplain Ron Padgett. The tall, husky young officer slowly walked toward me, shyly asking in a whisper if he should take Connie back to his cell. "No," I said, "not until he's ready." The young man nodded silently; after taking a couple of steps toward the case manager's office, he turned back around. With downcast eyes, he shook his head slowly and sighed deeply. "I couldn't tell my mother goodbye—not like this," he said in a hushed voice. "Y'all would just have to drag me off." I grimaced, and whispered back to him, "Me, too."

Not a word had passed between Connie and his mother for a very long time. They just stood in the lobby, clinging tightly to each other in a long, final embrace. The frail-looking woman wept softly, her shoulders heaving. Connie gently patted her on the back, quietly telling her everything would be okay. "Don't cry, Mama. I'll always love you." With those words, Connie Ray Evans let go of his mother and let me know he was ready to go back to his cell. As the steel door slid open, Connie's brother and sister took their mother by the arm and stepped toward the entranceway. She stopped and looked up at me, the pain and torment of the moment etched on her brow. My mind drifted back to a book I had read many years earlier, one written by a prison warden of another era. I vividly recalled his assertion that the most difficult task he had ever performed was to witness the parting of a loving mother from a son who was about to be executed. Looking down into the kindly face of the woman who stood just inches away, I had not the slightest idea of what I should say. "I'm sorry" seemed logical, but it sounded too trite and routine as I repeated it over and over in my mind. Before I could say anything, Connie's mother reached out and gently rested her hand on my arm. "Mr. Cabana," she asked quietly, "do you have children?" I opened my mouth, but nothing came out—no words, no sound of any kind. Finally, biting my lip, I just nodded my head. Her eyes pleading and her voice trembling as her hand grasped mine, she said, "Please, sir, please don't kill my baby. Don't take my child away from me."

I had never experienced the kind of sinking feeling that I had at that moment. My eyes shifted to Dwight Presley and Chaplain Padgett, as if searching for an answer, even a simple clue. "Please," the woman tearfully repeated, "you don't have to do this, do you? Don't kill my baby." Slowly I managed a nervous, "I'm sorry," stammering and shifting uncomfortably as I spoke. I realized that Connie had been right after all. Waiting until Tuesday night to bid his mother good-bye would have just made things worse for everyone concerned.

If Connie Ray Evans was some awful monster deemed worthy of extermination, why did I feel so bad about it, I wondered. It has been said that men on death row are inhuman, cold-blooded killers. But as I stood and watched a grieving mother leave her son for the last time, I questioned how the sordid business of executions was supposed to be the great equalizer. I watched Connie's family slowly make their way to the parking lot, attempting to console each other over their private grief. "Is there ever an end to the pain?" I asked aloud, to no one in particular.

I walked to my car, questions and doubt flooding my mind. With increasing skepticism, I asked myself what I was doing in corrections and what my proper role was, questions for which there were no easy answers. When I returned home that midsummer afternoon, I embraced my wife and children for a long time. Watching Connie Evans and his mother say farewell suddenly made life seem so much more fleeting and vulnerable. That Sunday afternoon, I was reminded of how special my family was.

Monday came and went without incident. Connie's attorneys were still attempting to find some last-minute legal maneuver that would delay the inevitable. That afternoon I spoke with two aides to Gov. Bill Allain, asking that the governor consider a reprieve. They protested that there were no legal grounds to justify invoking executive clemency. Besides, it was too early for the governor to consider intervening; all legal avenues had to be exhausted before he would even entertain the idea. Even though Mississippi's chief executive needed no legal grounds to stop an execution, he was not about to incur the public's wrath without overwhelming legal justification. That meant that he would not discuss the matter until late Tuesday night. There was at least one hopeful sign though, however slight. Unlike a lot of states, Mississippi had no pardons board to hear such cases—the decision regarding executive clemency rested squarely with the governor. Bill Allain would likely meet with Evans's attorneys and family members to hear any arguments they wished to present concerning a reprieve. Before making a final decision, the governor would ask for my input: What kind of prisoner had Evans been? Was he likely to kill again, if spared from execution? In the final analysis, Connie's fate would come down to the human condition. He had, after all, admitted to the murder, and there was little for the lawyers to work with in the form of legal technicalities.

Tuesday, July 6, arrived, a typically sunny and hot day in the Delta. In a way, tired of fighting the demons of another sleepless night, I was glad to see daylight come. I spent most of the day on the row, talking with Connie as well as other inmates and staff. Evans had asked me if I would allow him to spend a little time with another of the men on death row—they wanted to read the Bible and pray. The request was a bit unusual, but it seemed harmless enough. I was reminded by an ever diligent security supervisor that it could be part of a plan to escape or create a disturbance of some kind, maybe even the taking of hostages in a desperate attempt to halt the execution. His warning was both appropriate and appreciated, but I chose to grant Evans his request.

Death row was full of quiet activity. Chaplains and counselors were there, and would be for the next couple of days, for all who might need them—whether inmate or staff. Parchman's psychologist, Mike Whelan, came around, checking on the condemned prisoner's mental state and asking Connie if he wanted any kind of medication to help calm him that night. (Connie refused the offer, and he seemed to be mentally quite sound.)

Tuesday afternoon I spoke for several minutes with Governor Allain. He was preparing for a possible meeting later in the evening with Connie's representatives. I had agonized for the past twenty-four hours over what I might say to the governor if presented with the opportunity. After all, there was nothing I could do that would make Connie Ray Evans any less a murderer. That was fact, established beyond any reasonable doubt; the best I could hope for was to present the human side. Governor Allain and I had discussed the death penalty during one of his visits to the penitentiary, and, though he never firmly expressed opposition to it, I sensed that he was not terribly excited about it, either.

I told the governor that I was absolutely convinced that Connie Ray Evans would never kill again, and that he would present no threat to other inmates if his sentence were commuted to life. "You're not asking me to execute the same man who came in here six years ago," I pointed out. Evans had arrived on death row a streetwise drug abuser, bitter and scornfully contemptuous of authority. He had changed, and I personally had watched the change, especially over the past three years. "Isn't that what prisons are supposed to be about," I asked Governor Allain, "change?" I continued to press my case, assiduously trying against all odds to convince him that Connie had earned a second chance. I emphasized repeatedly that the condemned murderer entertained no hope of ever walking among free people again. He was not asking for, nor did he pretend to have, a right to be free. He just wanted another chance at life.

Why should the taxpayers support him in prison for the rest of his life, the governor inquired skeptically. I fired back (respectfully, of course) that there were other men incarcerated in Parchman whose crimes were far worse than Connie's, men who were not even on death row. It was just a matter of luck, and lawyers, and all that. I was losing, and I knew it; I was not good enough, persuasive enough to be arguing for another man's life. Frustrated, I implored the governor to consider the fact that Evans had a partner in his crime. True, Connie was the triggerman, but the other guy was just as culpable under Mississippi's murder-felony law. But it was a familiar scene. Connie's partner ran straight to the prosecutor. Answer a few questions here, get a little reduction in the charge there, and the result was predictable: Connie Ray Evans received the death penalty, and his buddy got a twenty-year sentence, with all but five years suspended. He'd already been released by this time.

After a few more perfunctory questions, Governor Allain concluded our conversation by telling me he would notify me later in the evening, once he had made up his mind. There was no way, I thought, that the governor would grant executive clemency. In all fairness, there were several factors that could lead him to decide against Connie. He had to deal with the real world of politics and public opinion. He could not overlook the extremely strong public support in Mississippi for the death penalty. Before being elected governor, Bill Allain had been the state's attorney general, and he could not easily explain pursuing the death penalty against Evans in one office and granting executive clemency in another. Besides, commuting Connie's prison term to life meant he would be eligible for parole after serving ten years, for Mississippi had no provision for a sentence of life without parole. No governor would be willing to commute a death sentence, only to see the convict back on the streets within a few years. As the call came to an end, however, the governor's final words before hanging up offered just a bit of encouragement and satisfaction: "If I were up there, darned if I wouldn't want you on my side."

The conversation had shed little light on what Governor Allain might do. His reaction to my comments was fairly reserved and tight-lipped. I knew only too well, though, that it had not been enough; there just was not much to argue with. While I tried to assure the governor that I did not take lightly the business of recommending executive clemency, I fully realized that everyone else, except his family and friends, knew Connie Ray Evans as a cold-blooded murderer. I had come to see a different side to him, but it was a side that was unfamiliar to judges, lawyers, and governors.

Connie had made it easy for me to violate my rule of never getting too close to an inmate. I permitted myself to know him as a person, not just another prison number. He did not even fit the description of the "typical" death row murderer that most people carry in their minds. He did not spend six years on the row claiming to be innocent, nor did he sit in a cell for a few years and then suddenly experience a miraculous religious conversion. Oh, he was bitter and resentful at times, especially about the guy who committed the crime with him. Connie did not wish the death penalty on his cohort; he just had a difficult time understanding why he was not entitled to the same kind of second chance as the other man. Connie was also somewhat unusual in not being the type of prisoner who wore his religion on his sleeve—whatever the religious values he had come by while on the row, he kept them very private. Most odd about him, however, as inmates go, was that he largely accepted responsibility for his actions. He did not blame his crime on alcohol or other drugs, bad parents, or lousy schoolteachers. Just weeks earlier he had gone out of his way to tell me that "didn't nobody but Connie Ray Evans put Connie Ray Evans in here. I just wish I knew why."

By five o'clock Tuesday evening there had been no word from the U.S. Supreme Court, where his petition had been filed, and therefore nothing from the governor, either. Death row cases often go right down to the wire, and convicts sometimes receive a stay only after they have been taken to the death site. I left Connie for a short while to go home and have dinner with my family. At five-thirty I was interrupted by a knock on the door. Dwight Presley delivered a faxed message that had just arrived from the clerk of the United States Supreme Court. In the matter of *Evans v. Cabana*, the Court had denied the plaintiff relief. "That's it, it's all over," I said, trying to mask my disappointment with a matter-of-fact air. Getting up slowly, I loosened my tie, and I asked Dwight to call down to death row and advise Evans's attorney of the Supreme Court's decision.

There was no real eagerness on my part to return to Little Alcatraz; things grew more depressing with each passing hour. Anyway, I wanted Connie's attorney to have time to talk to him about the Court's decision. I found myself recoiling, wanting to withdraw from the process as much as I could. The closer midnight came, the more impersonal I wanted things to be. Maybe it would all be easier that way. On his way out the door, however, Dwight turned and spoke in an uncharacteristically subdued manner. "He wants to know if you're coming back. He wants to see you." I was tired and felt as though every bone in my body ached. "Yeah, I'll be back. God knows I don't want to, but I'll be back."

I arrived back on the row a short while later and found Connie in a surprisingly good frame of mind. His attorney had met with him, and he knew now that the governor was his last hope. However, he had already pretty much resigned himself to his fate.

At 8:00 P.M., Governor Allain notified me that there would be no executive clemency. There was nothing left to do but begin final preparations for the execution. Still seeming quite calm and relaxed, Connie asked to talk with Chaplain Ron Padgett for a while, and I took the opportunity to wander through the rest of the death row unit. Here and there, inmates were conversing in hushed voices with chaplains and counselors. For the most part, though things were quiet, the air was tense with anticipation. Word had circulated quickly among staff and inmates that Connie's clemency appeal had been denied by the governor, and a distinctly subdued attitude pervaded the row.

Shortly before he died, Connie and I had our last real conversation alone, except for a few private seconds in the chamber itself. He was very introspective, and his twenty-seven-year-old features seemed tired from the long fight. Now anxious to get it over with, he said, without warning: "I've caused so much pain to so many people. I never meant to kill that man. Right now, I don't know why I did. You know, I was taught to believe that when you die, if you go to heaven, anything you ever wanted to know, all you've gotta do is ask. Well, I think I'm goin' to heaven, 'cause I've been forgiven by the Lord. So in one way, I'm looking forward to getting this over with. You know why, Mr. Cabana? Because I'm going to ask why I did what I did. I just have to know."

I had run out of things to say. I was smoking one cigarette after another, barely putting out one before lighting the next. The Johnson execution had been difficult, but putting Connie Ray Evans to death had turned into a personal hell. I surprised myself, though, by blurting, "When you get up there, son, put in a good word for me." It seemed like the first time I had seen him smile in days. "I will, Mr. C. You can count on it." That little exchange seemed to lighten the air a bit, taking some of the morose edge away. Connie sat on his bunk, silent for a couple of minutes, lost in his thoughts. Without looking up, he asked if I could explain something he had always wondered about.

"How come y'all always do these things so late at night? Is it so the other guys won't get all riled up and stuff? I always figured it was to try and hide it, you know? Everyone else out there is asleep, so you just do it and in the morning no one knows the difference."

I hesitated, but only for a moment. Too late for secrets, I thought. "Nope, nothing as elaborate as that," I replied. "It's just a legal thing. If you happen to get a last-minute stay, then the state's got until midnight tomorrow to get it overturned and carry out the execution."

After laughing slightly and shaking his head, Connie looked me square in the eyes. "Ain't that funny?" he mused. "See, I happen to believe that when I die, I'm going to a better place. I guess the way y'all see it, you're just killing me at midnight. But for me, it's just the opposite. It's going to be like a sunrise on a whole new life. A midnight sunrise, you know?" His voice betrayed the emotion of the moment.

Telling him I would return soon, I walked outside into the humid July night. Looking up at the cloudless sky, I wondered when Connie Evans had last been able to see the moon and the stars, to feel the early morning dew, or to smell the freshness after a rain. There would be no more chances for the man who waited inside. "Please don't kill my baby." His mother's words would not leave my head. Not loud, not hysterical—just the soulful words of a heartbroken mother.

The outside door to the execution room was open, and as I stood in the darkness I could see inside the open chamber. There it was—the "black death," sitting silent and impassive in the middle of the chamber. I was convinced that it was waiting, somehow knowing that before the

The open door reveals the inside of the gas chamber. Behind the chair can be seen the metal pole that caused such an uproar during the execution of child killer Jimmy Lee Gray.

night was over still another victim would be taken into its deathly embrace. I stepped back inside the building, where an air of expectancy weighed on everyone. Don Holcutt and Roger Vanlandingham assured me that everything was ready, asking once again what time the prisoner would be brought into the chamber. "Twelve o'clock, not a minute earlier," I responded crisply. Barry Parker and Fred Childs were busy checking the straps and headrest on the chair one last time. Mentioning to Fred that I had filled Evans in on how things would go and what to expect, I asked him to perform one more chore. "Before you step out of the chamber, after you've got him strapped in the chair, maybe you could just tell him one more time about breathing." Childs responded, "Yes, sir," and went on about his business.

Behind me, Dwight Presley was on the phone, relaying some information to the administration building, where a horde of media people were gathered. Raymond Roberts stood next to Presley, clipboard in hand. Raymond, who had served very ably as my deputy superintendent, had since been promoted to superintendent of a prison in Jackson. I had asked him to come back to Parchman and log every detail connected with the execution. His clipboard held a single sheet of paper that contained spaces for listing the time the prisoner was brought into the chamber, the time the cyanide was dropped into the chemicals, the time the gas struck the prisoner's face, the time the prisoner lost consciousness, and every other detail that we could anticipate. A few feet away, in the far-right-hand corner of the room, the two attending physicians busied themselves with checking their equipment. Two long stethoscopes protruded through the wall of the chamber; these would be taped to Connie Evans's chest. The EKG monitor, also with two sets of leads, snaked through the chamber's wall as well.

Presley covered the phone with his hand long enough to tell me it was 11:15, time to move Evans to the last-night cell. I turned to Deputy Warden Steve Puckett, who was going over some mechanical procedures with Don Holcutt. Grimacing, Steve acknowledged my nod of instruction. Sliding his hands into his pants pockets, the tall, boyish-looking Puckett intoned in his deepest voice, "Time to walk the last mile."

Fred Childs, Barry Parker, and Dwight Presley followed Steve and me as we stepped out into the cellblock. The officers on the block were closing the windows along the top of the tier. The heavy old steel-framed windows made a loud noise as they were slammed shut one by one. Each time I heard the noise echo up and down the tier, my skin crawled and I jumped just a little. The electric lock released the door at the end of the tier with a crack. Everything seemed magnified—every sound, every whisper. Though it was only a few feet to the cell where Connie had spent the last seventy-two hours, I moved more slowly than usual.

My feet were heavy, I felt as though I had to force my legs to move, and I could feel my heart pounding in my chest. As I approached his darkened cell, Connie was exchanging a final good-bye with his attorney. Chaplain Ron Padgett, standing just to my right, patted me on the shoulder. He knew how difficult this was for me, and I was glad he was there. Connie, who knew it was time, stood there expectantly, waiting for me to tell him. My knees were shaking and I could feel myself bathed in perspiration. All sound on the tier had ceased. Death row officers were crowded at the door at the other end of the tier, silently waiting for Connie Ray Evans to step out of his cell. They had worked with him, known him, for more than six years, and it was difficult for them, too. Just like me, many of the officers had come to understand another side of Connie (even though the unwritten rules said they should not). Just like me, they had neither forgotten nor excused what he did. But they did not forget that he was a human being, and they were hurting, too. Again the words filled my ears: "Please don't kill my baby. Don't take my child away from me."

"Jesus!" I exclaimed softly, out loud. Chaplain Padgett asked me if I was all right. After nodding affirmatively, I finally said quietly, "Connie, it's time to go, son." The cell door clanged, and up and down the tier inmates quietly exchanged final good-byes with the condemned man. One of the officers at the other end of the tier offered a sympathetic "Hang in there, Connie." I gently took the prisoner's arm, and asked Chaplain Padgett to walk on the other side. As we headed for the door leading to the last-night cell, a little way behind us an inmate began softly humming "Amazing Grace." Connie was trembling noticeably, and as we entered the alcove between the tier and the last-night room his knees buckled. I grabbed his left arm with both hands and asked him if he was okay. "I'm scared," he whispered hoarsely.

I looked at him in the dim light, as we retraced the steps I had walked with Edward Johnson just a few weeks earlier. The "last mile" seemed an eternity, every step a painful reminder of what waited at the end of the walk. Where was the cold-blooded murderer, I wondered, as we approached the door to the last-night cell. I had looked for that man before in Edward Earl Johnson, and I still had not found him—I saw, in my grasp, only a frightened child.

In the last-night cell, the terrible loneliness of it all began to make its presence felt more forcefully than ever. The chaplain sat on one side of the condemned man, while I sat nearest the chamber door. "Connie," I said softly, "I told Earl that we would get through this thing together, and I know that probably sounds strange. But it's true. We have to walk every step together, even the last one. A little piece of me died inside when Earl died. I know you probably can't understand that, but it's true."

Turning and looking intently into my eyes, Connie absolved me of any blame. "I know you have a job to do. I don't blame you, Mr. Cabana. I wish we could have known each other outside the prison. Who knows, under different circumstances, I might could've been your friend. God knows, you've been one to me."

"You are my friend, Connie," I responded, shaking. "I won't forget you."

Chaplain Padgett put his arm around Connie's shoulders, offering some words of encouragement and strength. I got up from the bunk and looked at my watch. I began to explain to Connie that in a few minutes a medical technician would come in to attach a couple of electrodes for the EKG monitor, and then it would almost be time. I had barely finished speaking when a knock sounded on the heavy metal door and a key turned in the lock. Otha Ferguson, a nurse, stepped in. Swiftly applying the two leads to Connie's chest, he wished him Godspeed and left the room. The door swung closed, the sound of heavy metal reverberating in the cramped room.

Looking like a forlorn child, Connie Ray Evans glanced toward me and asked if I would join him and Chaplain Padgett in a prayer. The three of us silently joined hands and recited the Lord's Prayer, after which Connie and Ron embraced. Turning to me, he managed a smile, and asked if it would be okay for a convict to hug the warden. "You bet it is," I said unabashedly. Moments later there was another loud knock, and I asked Connie if he was ready. The door to the chamber swung open, and, with my arm around his shoulders, I led him inside.

As if struck by a bolt of lightning, I suddenly realized that Dwight Presley had been telling me that everything was ready to proceed. I scanned the room, puzzled at why everyone was staring at me, until I realized how lost in my thoughts I had become. How long had I been standing there, trapped in my memories? I looked through the thick plate of glass at my prisoner, and then anxiously at the executioner.

"Let's do it," I said, the words only slightly more than audible. The executioner looked at me for a second. "Do it!" I said emphatically.

Almost immediately the lever dropped with a thunderous noise, sending its deadly payload of cyanide crystals into the chemicals beneath the chair. The EKG monitor fluctuated wildly, its beeping growing louder and louder. With Edward Johnson's execution still fresh in my mind, I knew only too well what to expect. As the executioner called out the time for Raymond Roberts to log, a cloud of poisonous gas began rising from the floor. My eyes were glued to Connie. He breathed very deeply several times in rapid succession; then, to my horror, he began holding his breath. No, I thought, you have to breathe. His fingers gripped the arms of the steel chair, and his teeth were clenched as if in a final act of defiance. I knew better, I knew it was the act of a man desperate to live, even in the face of inevitable death. The veins in his neck were nearly popping. *"Jesus Christ!"* I suddenly said aloud. *"Breathe! Dear God, Make Him Breathe!"* Almost at that instant the violent struggle began. Connie started to inhale in extremely rapid, short bursts. Suddenly his eyes rolled back, revealing nothing but white, then rolled forward again. They grew large, the size of silver dollars, and a wild look of fear engulfed his face. As I stood riveted to the scene inside, I silently prayed for it to be over quickly. Connie's muscles strained at every point up and down his body. He was beginning to drool from the corners of his mouth, his face twitching violently. I thanked God that we had installed the device to secure his head. Even strapped as firmly as he was, it was a violent, repulsive death. His chest heaved against the leather straps, his lungs trying desperately to gulp something besides the deadly gas that enveloped the entire chamber in a dense cloud. Thick, foamy, yellowish saliva began to pour from the corners and bottom of his mouth, and his nose exuded a runny, clear liquid. His eyelids repeatedly fluttered open and shut, as his eyes rolled back out of sight again. His feet strained against the floor, with his toes jerking violently upward. Still, his fingers scratched and clawed furiously at the chair's cold, steel arms. My own eyes were wet, and I tried wiping them with a handkerchief without anyone noticing. Somehow, it was worse than before, more violent than I had remembered.

I looked into the witness room. They had all become silent when the lever dropped. A few had a partial view of the prisoner from the side. None, however, could see what I saw. They could only imagine it.

Although the struggle seemed to go on forever, it was, in reality, over quickly. Connie's body, his fingers no longer glued to the chair, slumped, at least as much as the straps would permit. Now it was just a matter of waiting for technology to complete its task. The EKG monitor still registered considerable heart activity. It had taken barely a minute for Connie Ray Evans to lapse into unconsciousness.

As I looked at him sitting motionless in the chair, I noticed that his pants had a large wet spot. I knew, as I stood there trying to take in everything, that anyone else would think it silly of me, but I felt bad that he had urinated on himself. Connie did not want to do that, he did not want to be embarrassed. It was part of the degradation and humiliation, but there would be more. When he had been pronounced dead, and the cyanide fumes had been ventilated into the night air, officers in protective rubber gear and gas masks would enter the chamber. Unstrapping his body, they would lay him on the chamber floor and wash him down with a garden hose. His clothing would be removed and placed in plastic garbage bags for incineration. Then the coroner, without ceremony, would pronounce him dead. The corpse of Connie Ray Evans would be loaded into a waiting hearse.

After about eight minutes, while waiting for the EKG monitor to register an end to the heart activity, I was shocked by a loud noise from the chamber. Connie's body, without warning, became tense and rigid again, and his chest heaved as he appeared to take a very long, deep breath; as he did so, a loud, guttural noise filled the chamber. Horrified, I turned to Dr. Bennie Wright, utterly speechless. It could not be happening, I thought. Something had gone terribly wrong and he had not died! Now we would have to do it again. But the doctor quickly dispelled my fears. The movement and sounds were nothing more than normal, postmortem muscular reactions. I breathed a sigh of relief, although my pulse continued to race for a few more moments. Finally, some fifteen minutes after the gas first invaded Connie's lungs, the line on the EKG monitor flattened out and, mercifully, he was pronounced dead.

My wife was waiting for me outside the administration building. As I slowly got out of the car, she stepped off the sidewalk and took my hand. Before heading for the conference room, and a waiting press corps, I looked at her and shook my head. "No more. I don't want to do this anymore."

The press conference was typical of such events, the questions predictable. Finally, by two o'clock, the last of the reporters had left the institution and I was ready to go home. Physically exhausted and emotionally spent, I slumped at my desk, unable to get my mind off Connie Evans's mother. I had no way of knowing it that night, but within three months she would die of a heart attack. A few months later, his stepfather would succumb to cancer.

Fortunately, my family and I had planned on leaving for a brief vacation the next morning, my first real time off in several years. As I rose slowly to my feet, Dwight Presley asked what I was going to do on my break, besides take a much needed rest. "I think I'll call my mother," I replied wistfully.

As Miriam and I slowly walked home, a welcome breeze caressed our faces. We said nothing; we did not have to. Holding my hand tightly, she remarked how bright the moon was. Looking up at the sky above us, I thought it looked more beautiful than I had ever seen it before. And I felt just a little less lonely. Nestled in the night sky among the stars and wispy clouds was another of God's most wonderful creations, one I had never really appreciated before: a midnight sunrise.

Epilogue

Hattiesburg, Mississippi, 1995

Although it seems like yesterday, eight years have passed since the execution of Edward Earl Johnson and Connie Ray Evans. Following Connie's execution, I plunged back into my work with a sense of urgency. For a time, it must have seemed that I was pursuing my duties with a vitality and determination not seen before. In a very real sense, I was. Each new day's crises kept me from having to think or remember. But nothing could dispel the feelings I harbored inside. Try as I did, I could not remove the lingering doubt or bewilderment.

Despite having worked in corrections for nearly two decades, I suddenly felt like a stranger. A pall, which I felt powerless to rid myself of, had been cast over my job. For the first time, I found myself considering what life after corrections might be like. Of one thing I was certain—whatever the future might hold, I had privately concluded that I would not supervise another execution. As things turned out, no more convicts were put to death in Mississippi until 1989, by which time I had been able to leave Parchman without setting foot in the death house again.

Across the United States today, the move to restore capital punishment continues to gain momentum. More than three dozen states, and the federal government, have enacted death penalty laws. The number of executions continues to rise steadily as America uses the machinery of death more frequently than at any time since the 1930s. Every political candidate, whether for the county courthouse or the White House, wants to be seen as "tough on crime." Whether the method is gas or lethal injection or hanging or electrocution or firing squad, and regardless of the cost in dollars or human lives, the flames of the capital punishment solution are fanned by misleading political rhetoric and journalistic sensationalism.

Crime is, and should be, of grave concern to every right-thinking American. We are a people, however, in search of the quick fix, the simple solution, to a very complex problem. Only when we become serious about fighting poverty, child abuse, drugs, and a host of other scourges will we begin to make serious inroads on violent crime. Not until Americans return to the foundations of our past, where moral values and families reigned supreme, will we find the comfort and security that we long for.

I do not offer excuses for those who commit crimes. For every hard-luck story to be found in prison, there are many, many more people who overcame severe obstacles and made a place for themselves in society. On the other hand, however, fate often draws a thin line between the "keepers and the kept."

I was seldom surprised that the hundreds of condemned prisoners I worked with were on death row. But, when I had learned of their backgrounds and the sordid details of their so-called formative years, I was very often surprised that it had taken them as long as it had to get there. In many respects, they were no different from most "normal," law-abiding people, except for a bad break here or a different chance there.

This is not a particularly good time in which to find myself an opponent of capital punishment. Paradoxically, however, if this is the worst of times to be against the death penalty, it may also be the best of times. Never has there been greater need for rationality and clear thinking. Absent the emotionalism and histrionics that have always been so characteristic of the debate, the present offers greater opportunity then ever for pragmatism and calm deliberation. There is much need, and room, for both.

Facts on the Death Penalty

In 1996, thirty-eight states, the United States government, and the United States military impose the death penalty.

More and more states are turning to lethal injection as the preferred method of execution. A number of states still retain the gas chamber, electric chair, hanging, and firing squad as alternative methods of execution.

There have been 290 executions since 1976. The number of prisoners on death row in the United States exceeds 3,000.

California and Texas lead the nation in the number of condemned prisoners.

The United States is one of fewer than a half dozen nations that execute those convicted of capital offenses as juveniles. Since 1990, the United States has executed six juvenile offenders—more than any other country.

Since the death penalty was reintroduced in the United States in 1976, more than sixty condemned prisoners have been released from death row. They were wrongfully convicted and sentenced to die for crimes they did not commit.

Since 1900, there have been at least twenty-four documented instances of executions of innocent persons in the United States.

(These figures were provided by the National Coalition Against the Death Penalty and by Amnesty International.)

Index